K Smith
Jan 76

Managing Meetings

# MANAGING MEETINGS

# Barry Maude

BUSINESS BOOKS LIMITED
London

First published 1975

© BARRY MAUDE 1975

ISBN 0 220 66270 3

This book has been set 11 on 12 point Baskerville by Inforum of Portsmouth, prepared for press by The Ivory Head Press, 170 Murray Road, London W5 and printed in England by W & J Mackay Limited, Chatham by photo-litho, for the publishers, Business Books Limited, publishing offices: Mercury House, Waterloo Road, London SE1

# Contents

# Preface

Remarkable things happen when meetings are made more businesslike. More gets done in less time. Running costs are cut. *Better decisions are made.*

That's important. Because better decisions mean bigger profits.

Meetings can boost profits provided that they are well run. But according to one consultant, no more than one meeting in ten is run efficiently.

Why not make *your* meetings more businesslike — simply by applying the planning and control techniques described in this book?

* * *

Many people have contributed to make this book possible. I am especially grateful to all those people — managers and others — who discussed their experiences of meetings with me and, in some cases, allowed me to record and quote what they said.

I should like to thank David Grossman and Peter Hill for their support and enthusiasm all the way through; Mick Davis for his entertaining cartoons; Alan Law and Ivan Osbourne for their excellent photographs; and Alan Chatfield for the three-dimensional models used for Figures 1 and 17. I am grateful to GEC-Xpelair and to Charles Barker, Black & Gross, for permission to use the photographs of these models.

Ward Associates, who designed the board room of Beagle House, kindly supplied the photograph for Figure 18.

*One can do worse than think of a business organisation as a hierarchy of committees*

**John Kenneth Galbraith**

# Part 1
# MANAGEMENT MEETINGS

*In most companies meetings play a vital role, for the modern business battle is too big and complex for the captain of industry to fight alone. Ensemble management is in vogue, with the meeting as its most characteristic tool. That is why William Whyte has observed: 'For the young man on the make there is no better vehicle than the conference way'.*

# 1
# Why meetings matter

At Boeing two years ago during a serious slump, top managers began to meet for a few hours each day. The idea of these meetings was to pool ideas and knowledge so that ways of stimulating new business could be identified. The meetings worked. A whole range of exciting new ideas about *land* and *water* transportation took place. When developed and applied these helped to pull the company out of its nose-dive.

You still hear the cynics — a meeting is a meeting to decide when the next meeting will be held; a meeting is a group of the unfit appointed by the unwilling to do the unnecessary. But, when properly run, meetings do work. Indeed, the wheels of modern industry are turned by committees. This is because the business battle has become too big and complex for the captain of industry to fight alone.

The vital role of meetings in modern business is shown by the establishment of the lunch conference as an opportunity for making decisions and clinching deals. One executive — William Meese, President of the Detroit Edison Company — even holds daily *breakfast* sessions in the company cafeteria, and uses these informal meetings as opportunities to listen to the opinions and ideas of other managers.

The more complex a company becomes the more it relies on teamwork and coordination to solve its problems.* This is so especially in times of crisis in the organisation, when widespread discussion is needed to ensure maximum awareness of the company's problems and the range of possibilities.

Today a company's personnel and production policies, its marketing plans and advertising schedules and many other aspects of its operations are usually thrashed out in meetings. There are finance committees, production committees, joint consultative committees, progress meetings, supervisors' meetings, staff conferences.... How many thousands of meetings like this are held throughout industry every day?

This participative approach to management is not only popular (in the old days juniors used to see eye to eye with the boss only because they were glaring at each other), it is also efficient, for it gets more out of people by tapping their talents and experience. This, in turn, touches off production leaps and zippier growth. As Rensis Likert points out in *New Patterns of Management*:

> An organisation will function best when its personnel function not as individuals but as members of highly efficient work groups with high performance goals. Consequently, management should deliberately build these effective groups, linking them into an over-all organisation by means of people who hold overlapping group membership. The superior in one group is a subordinate in the next group, and so on through the organisation.

There is little room for superstars in this vision of ensemble management. Some of the most celebrated creative and professional figures of the past 50 years have shared this enthusiasm for teamwork. Gropius, for instance, wanted modern building to be the result of teamwork in which each member fully appreciated his contribution to the whole. Whereas most buildings are stamped with the personal-

---

* Burns and Stalker have reported [1.1] on the effect of organisational structure on electronics firms. In the rapidly changing environment of the electronics industry, firms with an 'organic' structure survived; those with a 'mechanistic' structure failed. In an organic organisation direct contact between individuals at different levels and free interaction between different specialists is allowed for. Lines of organisation are not rigidly structured and there are many informal meetings and discussions.

ity of the architect, Gropius preached 'the conquest of the cult of personality', exemplified in the foundation in 1945 in America of the group practice *The Architects' Collaborative*. Think too of the growth of the group practice in law, medicine and other professions.

## Ensemble management

Standards of what is efficient are changing. Human resources accounting is becoming the yardstick of corporate performance. Today, business grace depends on good works by the entire management team, not just the few top men. That is why, when a company's production goes through the roof after years of gentle stagnation, it is sometimes on the strength of this simple idea of participative management exploding in the board room. For instance, the British firm, Scott Bader, chalked up much higher sales after they opted for co-ownership and the group approach that goes with it. Perhaps more firms should experiment with this modern alchemy.

Autocratic management is an anachronism, completely out of synch with the super-democratic, utterly liberated Aquarian age that has arrived at the other side of the factory gate. (Why let the dictator's shadow kill the sparkle of our modern dream?) While autocratic management methods (the corporate equivalent of Stalinism) flatter the egos of the few top men, just how stultifying they can be for everyone else many a loss-laden annual report has shown. Usually they manage to produce high levels of frustration combined with a low level of accomplishment.

Everybody needs status. And the most telling measure of status in a company is the right to have a say in the decisions that are made. Certainly anyone who has squirmed beneath the thumb of an occupational dictator will cheer on those companies who have thrust forward to more participative styles of management — in effect, called more meetings. More and more companies seem to be doing so. Indeed, it is difficult to see how any organisation containing large numbers of interacting groups could get by *without* a lot of meetings. Perhaps the trend reflects the increase in the number of specialists.

Whatever the reason, even autocratic firms have their informal committees, with managers meeting over coffee to discuss production or marketing problems, and supervisors chatting in the canteen about new safety practices or overtime schedules. And in every firm at least one formal committee operates — the board of directors.

Autocratic managers see the need for helpers but not for other managers. But to survive in the modern business jungle even the hard-line manager needs to become adept at tossing liberal confetti — i.e. to let others have their say in meetings and elsewhere. Arthur Cohen, executive head of the Arlen Realty and Development Corporation has a brand of 'liberalism' that goes well beyond confetti-throwing. How's this for a picture of successful corporate management in action:

> He keeps an eye on the critical points of many projects, darting in and out of the ten conference rooms on the two executive floors at Arlen headquarters, which are almost always in use for some deal-hatching process. 'We call it the doctor's office, with all the consulting rooms', says one Arlen executive....[1.2]

## Twentieth-century man

If the nineteenth century was the age of the self-made man, the twentieth is the age of the committeeman. The reason is simple. Technological development means increasingly complex production processes. These require vast amounts of capital and sophisticated organisations to handle them. In these large and complex organisations, meetings and committees are often the only practical way of coordinating the many different functions and promoting communication between departments.

Most modern industrial problems are really compendiums of sub-problems with different experts handling different aspects. Day by day, information has to be exchanged and meetings called, so that gradually the team can work towards a solution — the plant is installed, the project developed, the order completed.

These facts of twentieth-century industrial life explain why meetings play an increasingly important role. Most companies depend on them for survival. For instance, that sprawling Japanese giant, Matsushita, holds itself together by a judicious combination of ancient (group harmony) and modern (widely dispersed decision-making and the plethora of meetings that goes with it). Informal meetings are the main method used by the company's executives for communicating with each other. The monthly meeting for the 200 top managers (always preceded by a coffee hour to promote harmony) is felt to be an essential forum for discussing new plans and opportunities and for letting each part of the company know what all the other parts are doing.

## Tiny brain, outsize body

Admittedly, a few corporate tyrannosauri have blundered into the mid-70s from an earlier age and still exist, dead but intact. In these firms a single 'strong man' at the top spurns meetings and committees and takes all the decisions himself. It's the olde and ultimately tragick tale of the tiny brain and outsize body. (This combination is commoner than we sometimes like to think: remember that a healthy beast may be no more than a sick beast unaware of its condition.) However, in most other firms managers at all levels can participate in meetings and so make their talents available to the whole organisation. And not only the organisation benefits. For participation in decision-making increases a member's understanding of the decision and his commitment to it. The individual grows — and a better job gets done.

William Whyte has, somewhat satirically, described the 'conference way' of self-improvement:

> For a young man on the make there is no better vehicle than the conference way...via the conference he can expose himself to all sorts of superiors across the line of command. Given minimum committeemanship skills, by an adroit question here and a modest suggestion there, he can call attention to himself and still play the game.[1.3]

How many managers lack even minimum committeemanship skills?

Imagine that you are an engineer working for a construction company and that you have worked out a scheme for reducing demolition costs by at least 5 per cent. You collect a lot of evidence to support your case — expert testimony, statistics and so on. You hand in a report to your boss. Only one obstacle remains: the company's Operations Committee, which must be convinced before your scheme can be placed before the board.

You go into the committee meeting and more or less throw your case at the members, confident that the facts will speak for themselves. Your contribution to the following discussion is confined to restating points already made in your opening statement. Yet you're hurt and surprised when the committee reject your proposal.

An opportunity to reduce costs has been lost, and your personal reputation has suffered. Yet a year later the same committee accepts a very similar scheme presented (expertly) by another man.

It's a real-life story, and the experience is probably a fairly common one. For often the facts refuse to speak for themselves and only skilled committeemanship can ram home their significance. A polished presentation can sway even the toughest committee. In spite of the Roskill Commission's recommendations, the British Cabinet — the most important committee in the country — decided to site London's new airport at Foulness, largely because of the brilliant presentation of its case by the anti-Cublington lobby. (That was before another British Cabinet cancelled the Foulness project — partly because of effective campaigning by conservationist groups.) But excellent proposals die the death when presentation is weak.

## Why meetings matter

Here are some good reasons why a manager needs to train himself in committee skills:

1   *Being involved in meetings sharpens people's feelings for the business as a whole*, and so develops them for more responsible jobs. 'Serving on committees', one executive reported, 'forces me to organise my own thinking about what goes on in the company and to dig up facts to support the conclusions I reach'.

2   *Subordinates willingly support decisions they have helped to make.* Bavelas found that lecturing, ordering or appealing to workers were all ineffective ways of stimulating production, but that production rose steadily once a group decision had been reached in a meeting. Remember, too, that top management is more likely to accept decisions arrived at by group process.

3   *Group discussion is a powerful tool of persuasion.* A skilled committeeman can persuade people to think again and get proposals accepted where his less experienced colleagues fail.

4   Sooner or later the attitudes and goals of a manager or administrator working independently become frozen: *but a committee can be far more flexible in its thinking* because the membership is con-

tinuously changing and members are continuously influencing each other.

5 *Committees become relatively more efficient with time*:
   — Individuals learn to work together as a team.
   — The committee accumulates a body of collective wisdom in which all the members share and which remains even if some members leave. It is available to new members as a guide and teaching aid.
   — Committees gradually improve on their organisation and procedure, which allows problems to be solved faster.

Antony Jay has described how membership of a group can weld a number of diverse individuals into an effective task force:

   I could brief a *Tonight* director or reporter on the treatment of a film story in a few minutes, whereas with an equally skilled professional who had never worked with us it would have taken an hour's discussion and been far less clear at the end...we had argued over the right and wrong ways in hours of doctrinal discussions based on hundreds of films and so we all knew the pitfalls too well to have to talk about them.[1.4]

Members of any committee to some extent develop the same outlook, and this increases the speed and accuracy of communication between them, both in and out of meetings.

**Group or solo decision ?**

A manager in a Yorkshire wool mill is asked to draw up a list of redundancies. He calculates that eventually 60 men can be made redundant without affecting productivity. He presents his report to the managing director who studies it, then looks at him sourly. 'Now look, lad, I know these men aren't needed, but we can't make them redundant.'

   'Why not, sir ?'

   'Because, lad, they're my bloody brass band.' Bowing low, the manager crawls from the presence.

   The managing director made his decision because nobody dared to tell him he was being a bloody fool. If he had had to explain his intention to a meeting of senior managers, no doubt a salvo of blunt comments or, at least, hints and loaded questions would have made him think again.

Having to present intentions — and results — to committees applies a crude but salutary pressure to the complacent or wrong-headed executive. That, in the last resort, is why Henry Ford encourages his own board of directors to criticise him: 'I have to talk with the board about my performance, whether I'm emphasising the right things. I've always told them quite openly that if the time ever comes when I should step down, they ought to tell me.'

*Meetings are good for you. They stop you making silly decisions. They force you to look more deeply into problems. And they force you to re-examine your own assumptions and first principles, as Kurt Lewin proved.* During the Second World War he had the job of persuading people to eat more liver, kidney and hearts. When people came together in discussion groups they were forced to re-examine their prejudices and, in many cases, they actually changed their diets.

The bigger the decision the greater the risk in permitting one man to make it. Consider, for instance, the cautionary tale of the Abu Dhabi banknotes. A decade ago, one man, Sheik Shakbut, made all the important decisions. One of these was to store all the banknotes of the tiny sheikhdom in a back room of the palace. It worked out well until somebody noticed that rats had nibbled away several cubic yards of the crisp and crinkly pile.

Soon afterwards, a *committee* was set up, with members drawn from international banking circles, to make important financial and investment decisions. Perhaps the most important thing the committee did was to prevent any one individual taking silly decisions — with the result that, since then, Abu Dhabi's reserves have been piling up at a rat-exhausting pace.

Meetings generally make fewer errors than individual decision-makers, and the errors they do make are more quickly detected (because of interaction between different and mutually critical types of people). Other advantages of group decision making are:

1   Groups forecasts and judgements are more likely to be on target than individual judgements because of the effect of averaging.
2   Meetings generate more ways of tackling the problem.
3   Decisions taken in a meeting are likely to be implemented energetically by the members.
4   The presence of others stimulates a sense of commitment in the members, who formulate their ideas and prepare their proposals more carefully than if working alone.

Pelz found that optimum performance is associated with *(a)* consulting some colleagues whose orientation differs from one's own — who challenge one's views and point out shortcomings — and *(b)* consulting some colleagues who share one's orientation and who support and develop one's ideas [1.5]. In most meetings, both kinds of consultation occur simultaneously.

Committees and meetings are also effective means for dealing with sudden crises in the organisation. You can win people's cooperating, quickly collect a lot of ideas for action and inform people what steps are being taken to deal with the crisis.

**Where committees score**

Committees score over individual executives when handling the following kinds of problem:

*1 Problems that have many different facets or problems that require skills or information from different specialists,* for example a marketing plan or a building project. Often the best way to tackle a problem of this kind is to split the meeting into sub-groups and divide the problem into its component parts. Each sub-group then focuses on that aspect that it is best qualified to handle.

*2 When a decision requires judgment rather than calculations or expertise,* and especially when an averaged or collective judgment is more likely to be on target than a single individual's: for example — How long will it take to complete a development project? What is the present state of labour relations in the company? (When individuals are asked to judge the temperature of the room or the number of pebbles in a jar their estimates tend to be scattered symmetrically around the true value. The averaged *group* judgment, on the other hand, I have always found to be very accurate.) In meetings, different members can point to bias and blind spots in each other's estimates, which reduces the chances of gross error in the collective judgment or decision.

*3 When a pooling of ideas improves the chances of a good decision:* for example, ways of improving safety procedures, finding new customers or developing new products.

*4 When the most important consideration is the members' accept-*

*ance of the decision,* as when deciding holiday or overtime schedules, or which employees should be issued with new tools, etc.

Generally, meetings are more willing to take risky decisions than
individual decision-makers. This 'risky shift phenomenon' (aca-
demia's pretentious label), may stem from diffuse responsibility, or
simply from the rhetorical punch packed by risk-taking individuals
in meetings. Thus meetings may have a particularly valuable part
to play whenever bold new initiatives are needed to lift a company
over its problems.

## When not to call a meeting

Never call a meeting when an individual decision-maker would get
better results. Generally, individuals are better than meetings at
dealing with the following kinds of problem:

1   *Simple routine problems,* such as approving small items of
expenditure, drawing up work rosters, and the like. Kelley and
Thibaut suggest [1.6] that both very easy problems and very difficult problems are best handled by individuals.

2   *Problems with a 'correct' answer that a technical expert can
solve,* such as a costing or pricing problem, or the kind of machinery required. In cases like these a decision by majority vote or consensus might easily be the wrong one and cost the company a lot of
money. When a committee decision is required for statutory reasons, follow the example of the local authorities: delegate a technical expert or an official to deal with the problem and present his
recomendations to the committee for its approval.

3   *Problems where it is difficult or impossible to demonstrate the
correctness of any particular solution to the other members:* for
example, a new product design, an advertising media plan, or a
design for a more efficient office layout. Problems of this kind
should be handed over to an expert because discussion in a meeting
may only cloud the issue. If you don't immediately see the answer to
the following problem, for instance, no amount of discussion will
convince you:

> A man bought a horse for $60 and sold it for $70. Then he
> bought it back for $80 and again sold it for $90. How much
> money did he make in the horse business?

4   *Research indicates that subtle reasoning problems are generally performed more accurately by individuals than by meetings.* No doubt that is why about half of all patent inventors are individuals working without organisational support. Examples of problem-solving loners are Whittle (jet engine), Sikorsky (heicopter) and Anschutz-Kaempfe (gyrocompass). The great danger of presenting difficult reasoning problems to meetings to solve is that the competent members (those who know how to solve the problem) may be out-voted or even convinced by the rest. This might easily happen, for example, if this problem were presented to a meeting:

A:  Some Communists are advocates of heavy taxes
B:  All advocates of heavy taxes are Conservatives
Therefore:
1   Some advocates of heavy taxes are not Communists
2   Some Communists are Conservatives
3   Some Conservatives are Communists
4   Some Communists are now advocates of heavy taxes
5   None of these conclusions follows

Taylor, Berry and Block [1.7] found that groups of four working independently threw up better ideas than the same number working as a group. While Marquart [1.8] assumes that any individual with the qualities required to solve the problem would have solved it whether working alone or in a meeting. This implies that the quality of decision-making in a meeting is determined by the ability of its most competent member. If this is so, the practical implications are considerable. For instance, perhaps the quickest and cheapest way of improving a *committee's* problem-solving is to train *individuals* in problem-solving techniques.

The ideas of the foregoing section are tabulated for convenience in Table 1.


## Mr Average Executive

In the past, the exploited many have sweated for the idle few. In the future, the masses will grow fat and lazy with leisure while a corps of top executives works overtime. It's the wise executive who, deciding against ulcers, leaves some of the decisions to his committee colleagues.

It's the indispensable man who makes himself dispensable.

A report in the *Harvard Business Review* reveals the importance of meetings to executives. After examining replies to a question-

## Table 1

---

Advantages of meetings

---

1  Meetings get more out of people by tapping their talents and experience.

2  Meetings generate more ideas than a single individual.

3  Group judgements are likely to be more on target than individual judgements because of the effects of averaging.

4  Meetings make fewer gross errors than individuals.

5  Subordinates enthusiastically implement decisions they have helped to make.

6  Group pressure forces executives to look more deeply into problems and to re-examine their own predjudices.

7  Committees are generally more flexible in their thinking than individuals because members influence each other and membership is constantly changing.

8  Meetings curb the power of top executives.

9  As the members learn to work together as a team, the committee becomes more and more efficient.

10 Meetings are an essential device for coordinating the efforts of different specialists.

---

naire sent to subscribers, the journal reported:

> Mr Average Executive spends nearly 3½ hours a week in committee meetings; serves on three committees . . . finds an average of seven fellow executives sitting with him on each committee, and wishes there were only four others. Generally, each of his committees meets about every two weeks.
>
> In addition to these formal committee meetings, he spends the equivalent of one working day a week . . . in informal conference and consultation with fellow executives . . . .

## Advantages of decision-making by individuals

1 Individual decision-makers handle small, routine problems more efficiently and more cheaply than meetings

2 Only individuals can solve very subtle reasoning problems - for example, when it would be impossible to demonstrate the correctness of a particular solution to all the members of a meeting.

3 In a meeting, the quality of decision-making may be determined by the ability of its ablest member. When this is the case, the correct tactic is to identify this man and ask him to solve the problem alone.

4 Decisions by individuals are much cheaper - and generally faster - than group decisions.

5 Taking decisions alone develops executives for higher responsibility.

6 In some very small companies the boss is able to coordinate all activities in his own mind and should, therefore, take all the decisions.

7 In one experiment, when groups of four split up and each man worked independently, they threw up better ideas than when working together as a group.

Committees are considered important devices for sharing information, cross-fertilising ideas, and promoting coordinated management. While there are some executives who would allow committees to vote decisions and make policy, there are many more who prefer that committees recommend and advise the executive held responsible for the decision — frequently the chairman of the committee.

Meetings are big business these days. And every manager needs a good knowledge of the techniques for successfully running them

*Presenting plans to meetings is like exposing your ego to a grinding wheel*

and participating in them. Some of these techniques are described in the following chapters.

The captain of industry marched out of the text books two or three decades ago. Today, corporate efficiency depends more on ensemble management, whose basic tool is the meeting. In most large companies, major problems *have* to be taken by meetings because that may be the only practical way of coordinating the many different skills required for large-scale projects.

Meetings are good for you. Presenting your plans and results to a meeting is like exposing your ego to a grinding-wheel: it's painful, but it hones away the rough edges.

Meetings are a talent-tapping device, and participating in them sharpens people's feelings for the business as a whole and so develops them for greater responsibility. As Professor Galbraith points out:

> One can do worse than think of a business organisation as a hierarchy of committees . . . Association in a committee enables each member to come to know the intellectual resources and the reliability of his colleagues. Committee discussions enable members to pool information under circumstances which allow, also, of immediate probing to assess the relevance and reliability of the information offered. [1.9]

These are some of the reasons why meetings matter.

*The greatest communication barriers in
industry are those between management and
the work-force — because of different goals,
responsibilities and backgrounds. But the
barriers, however formidable, can be overcome when the two sides meet and talk about
their differences. That is why managers
should be eager to discuss their plans and policies with such over-age whipping-boys as
the shop steward and the union official. He
who consults achieves a healthier climate —
and higher productivity.*

# 2
# Meeting the employees

An engineering firm's management which in previous years had met union officials only at times of crisis decided to ask the union to meet them regularly, reason or no reason. So once a week the two sides met — just sat and talked informally. For the first time each found itself listening to the other. In a relaxed atmosphere each side was able to explain is point of view — and to learn the other side's.

Each meeting brought a quick exchange of pieces that brought both sides closer to their common objective — compromise, and therefore stabilitye across the industrial board.

When the number of disputes in the factory dropped management linked this with these informal meetings. Thus the meetings soon paid for themselves many times over.

When people from the two sides of industry sit round the same table they begin to understand one another's viewpoint. When they sit round the table long enough and often enough they even begin to share the same values and talk the same language. This, presumably, was the assumption when Ford of Europe held meetings recently with union representatives from Ford plants in Britain, Germany, France and Belgium, with the aim of reaching agreement on production policy and job security throughout Europe.

Think of how consultative meetings in the British coal mines in Lord Robens' time made possible the full merchanisation and the planned closure of more than 500 pits. And Sir William Swallow has said that he avoided serious strikes at Vauxhall while he was its head because of numerous meetings with the unions which enabled him to mop up grievances 'in minutes or hours'.

Of course, the grievances will remain unless employees feel that their bosses are *listening* during these meetings and will take action as a result of what they hear. Management itself has much to gain from listening, for it will gain the kind of grapevine information that is needed for decision-making.

### Experience-tapping

Another reason for listening in joint meetings is that employees have their own special work methods. They find short cuts. They develop quicker and easier ways of doing the job, like the machinist who boosted his output by making a short rod for steadying the cutting tool. By tapping this kind of know-how in joint meetings management can find ways of cutting operating and production costs. Westinghouse, for instance, reckoned that in one year it saved $1½ million through implementing ideas for technical improvements that stemmed from this kind of dialogue.

Matsushita, the giant Japanese company, hold regular 'free talks' between management and the employees, who are encouraged to talk about working conditions, their bosses, company policy and anything else that they please. And any useful ideas that emerge are sent straight to the board. In this company, divisional heads spend only an hour or so a day at their desks: the rest of the time is spent meeting the employees in formal and informal discussions. Matsushita reckon that direct contact is the secret of good communication.

To get the maximum return from meetings with the employees

---

* Perhaps any individuals in a group *have* to talk the same language to satisfy an innate need to communicate with each other: 'the territorial singer can sometimes quickly adapt to a rival by matching its song pattern to that of the intruder . . . the European robin's instantaneous imitation of an invader's signal amounts to saying, "I am talking to you, invader of the moment!".' [2.1]

**Figure 1**   *Many managers prefer small informal get-togethers with their employees*

why not let *them* decide what to talk about? Thus the employees will be initiating communication, not merely giving feedback.

## Early-warning system

Meetings with the employees — or with their union representatives — can act as a kind of early-warning system allowing management to spot danger areas before they explode. For instance, in a Yorkshire wool mill sales had been low for several years. Low morale was reflected in high absenteeism and high labour turnover. Then a rumour began to the effect that a redundancy plan was being drawn up. The board decided to scotch the rumour and drew up a statement saying that all jobs were secure. But the rumours persisted. A week later the chief shop steward demanded full details of the redundancy scheme. One-way communication had failed.

Eventually the board hit on a more effective way of convincing the employees. A series of departmental meetings was called with at least one director attending each meeting. Everyone attending was handed a copy of the board's previous statement and employees listened as the director explained just what was meant by *this* point; what the facts were behind *that* statement.

Then it was the director's turn to listen while the employees expressed their fears and fired questions. These the director tried to answer, fully and frankly. As a result of these meetings confidence in management grew. The rumours dissolved. Productivity picked up. But the improved industrial relations climate was the most valuable effect of all.

When the two sides of industry are far apart, meetings can be effective bridge-builders.

Some managers even use meetings as devices for improving *customer* relations. Senior managers at Motorola, for instance, arranged a large number of small informal meetings with purchasers to find out what they thought about the company's products. The meetings uncovered disquiet about the clarity and colour quality of television sets. This information inspired the company to develop the first single button that adjusts five characteristics of colour tuning at a touch.

## Cleavage in social ethics

In the celebrated Hawthorne studies, Elton Mayo's team of researchers studied 14 employees who attached wires to switches. A steady 6000 units a day were produced though management were sure output should have been 7000 a day. Financial incentives were introduced: output stayed at 6000 a day. Mayo's team eventually discovered that the restrictive practice was based on the men's idea of a fair day's work. 'Rate-busters' (produced too much), 'chisselers' (produced too little) and 'squealers' (too friendly with the supervisors) were subjected to pressure until they conformed to the men's unwritten code.

Management's incentives were ineffective because they were based on middle-class standards — the managers' own standards of self-advancement. The men's own code of a fair day's work remained undiscovered because management never bothered to find out what it was — a classic case of communication failure.

One hundred and thirty years ago, Disraeli wrote about 'Two nations . . . as ignorant of each other's habits, thoughts and feelings, as if they were dwellers in different zones or inhabitants of different planets'. Today a cleavage in social ethics still exists, and it separates the manager from his work force. Managers and workers have been to different schools. They live in different parts of town, go to different pubs, rarely mix socially. Neither learns the other's point of view. How many communication breakdowns in industry spring from this underlying experience gap?

Perhaps nationwide comprehensive education would, after all, be the best long-term method of improving industrial relations in Britain and some other European countries.

Close cooperation between the two sides of industry during the three-day working week period in Britain in 1974 shows that the gap can be bridged. But too many managers still regard industrial relations as somebody else's business. Hugh Parker, head of McKinsey's consultancy operation in Britain, points out that 'people who manage don't identify themselves with the interests of the managed. They stay aloof — at arm's length from the workers.'

Many managers over-rely on formal communication links with employees. But as Glacier Metals discovered, good communication doesn't come simply from setting up formal committees. For the most valuable kind of communication happens *informally* — when a manager chats with employees in the dining room, or in coffee conferences, or while he is 'walking the job'.

The manager's biggest intangible asset is his ability to communicate informally. This explains the great emphasis placed on informal meetings and discussions by the great management thinkers — Mayo, Homans, Roethlisberger and others. (The formal communication network links *roles* in the organisation; the informal network linke *people*.)

## Small, informal meetings

Many employees freeze in large gatherings but come alive in small groups — as the head of a management services division discovered after calling several mass meetings of workers to explain new incentive schemes. Because of their size, these meetings were impossible to control and far more heat than light was generated. So he asked staff to select six representatives to attend a meeting which would be small enough for him to explain exactly what the new proposals would mean.

Because of the smaller size the meeting was informal in atmosphere and everybody could have his say. It was possible to explain the proposals in depth. As a result, the representatives became very involved in the plan and even started suggesting improvements. Once again, the small informal meeting proved to be a highly effective way of communicating with the shop floor.

Mass meetings aren't the style at the Johnson and Johnson factory in Camberley either. There, management communicates with production units via a chain of small meetings between (a) managers and foremen, (b) foremen and supervisors and (c) supervisors and workers. This system of small, informal meetings has proved its efficacy in passing information down the line time and time again. For instance, when Britain was working a three-day week because of the Arab oil embargo, it proved easy to keep the work force posted daily about how things were going.

These are just some of the reasons why many managers prefer small informal get-togethers with their employees instead of full-scale departmental meetings. William Keefe has said: 'The listening manager, because he listens well, has his mental stethoscope of the heartbeat of the organisation and can usually predict what changes are needed and will occur' [2.2]. And provided that he is willing to *listen*, the manager should learn far more from small informal sessions with his staff than from larger, more formal encounters. Moreover, subordinates often leave these smaller sessions with an increased sense of participation and well-being.

### Listening-meetings

The manager who can't or won't listen to his employees may lurch blindly from one top-heavy policy to another. Listening to employees or their representatives in meetings means that employees can bring their on-line experience to bear on company problems. As Mary Parker Follett pointed out nearly half a century ago, the man who works the machine is as expert about it in his way as the man who designs or the man who orders the machine. Thus policy should be based on the activity and experience of the whole factory.

And what better way of tapping this experience than by regular face-to-face discussion in meetings?

The higher a manager climbs the more he is cut off from detailed activity on the firing line. Unless he can create communication links he is bound to be left in the dark about what is happening at grass roots level. Some top-level managers interpret no news as good news. But the deathly hush may only be because the employee voice is being strangled.

Sound policy depends on thousands of feeder roots stretching into every nook and cranny of the organisation. Simply relying on official union channels for contact can be a bad mistake. For in many factories there is a sizeable communication gap between officials and the rank-and-file members: management may not get the true picture by listening only to the shop steward. And anyway, only highly specific grievances can be dealt with through official union channels — a new safety guard for a machine, the rate for a particular job — which means that unless management takes the initiative in creating alternative links, vast areas of common concern will never get discussed.

## Group sessions

One such alternative link is the group session, attended by the whole department or section, which can be an excellent way of improving upward communication and of winning acceptance for new plans and policies. The meetings should be as informal as possible so that even the most timid employees are encouraged to say what they think. In a relaxed atmosphere, management has the chance to explain its plans. The employees can voice their feelings and say how they think the proposed changes could best be carried out. Work can be discussed, improvements suggested and grievances and misunderstandings ironed out.

In meetings like this, once the group as a whole has accepted a new policy or work method, even awkward individuals quickly accept the new conformity. Kurt Lewin has pointed out that 'if the group standard itself is changed the resistance which is due to the relation between individual and group standards is eliminated'. Some men take great pride in defying their bosses, but they think twice before opposing their own workmates.

*But before employees will accept a new method they have to be given the chance to talk themselves into a change of attitude. A* roughly similar mechanism seems to operate in psychotherapy, which works best when the patient draws his own conclusions about his attitudes and behaviour. So why not tackle the problem of slack time-keeping by calling a group session, then inviting employees to discuss the advantages and disadvantages of punctuality. Alternatively, why not ask them to form a committee to decide their own starting and finishing times? Even chronic malcontents keep to new standards that their own workmates have fixed.

That is why Polaroid call employees into group sessions then ask *them* to decide what kind of new machinery to buy. At Parish Instruments, decisions like this are taken during informal meetings which are held on the factory floor during protracted tea breaks — with the managing director joining in. At Cadbury Schweppes' headquarters in the United States, management-employee meetings are held to discuss a wide range of company matters, including the company's profits and the chairman's last statement to the shareholders.

## Output restriction

Consider the value of meetings in overcoming output restriction. To the worker, this is a logical form of self-protection against unreasonable demands or possible redundancies. Any one-way attempts to convince individuals otherwise are always fiercely resisted. As one supervisor reported: 'We know our time studies for welders don't mean much. They can always fiddle around with the air pressure or the quantity of acetylene. They always find a way of speeding up or slowing down the operations by adjusting their tools.'

Employees will change their methods and raise output only when the work-group as a whole nods approval. The social nature of output restriction was underlined by an investigation in a workshop that showed that girls tended to work at the same speed as their friends.

To plough through this particular barrier a meeting is required. For instance, why not call the employees together and explain why a change of approach is needed — because of extra job security, perhaps, or as a way of boosting earnings. Then leave them to *talk themselves* into a change of attitude.

Admittedly, there are risks in doing this. For instance, the discussion might lead to a hardening of attitudes rather than a change.

But there is a mass of evidence that shows just how productive participative meetings of this kind can be. An instance of this is the experiment that was carried out in a toy factory where girls had complained about the speed of a moving belt carrying components for assembly. After the meeting, in which the girls were asked to decide what kind of arrangement they wanted, a control dial was fitted to the work bench so that the girls themselves could control the speed of the belt. The girls were very pleased and morale soared. And the average speed at which the girls themselves ran the belt was higher than the speed they had complained about.

## Participation as a control method

Bavelas compared groups of sewing machine operators in the Harwood company. One group was allowed to hold a meeting to decide its own production goals. The other group made no decisions and set no goals. This group failed to improve its performance whereas the first group boosted its production. Because it had decided to.

Managers in a metal plating factory tried to find ways of allocating work. Every suggestion was rejected as 'unfair' in some way. In desperation, management asked the girls themselves to solve the problem. So the girls called a meeting and quickly worked out job allocations that even management agreed were better than anything so far. The new arrangement was subsequently implemented — with great smoothness.

*Through participation, management can increase its control by seeming to relinquish it:*

> Groups that participate in setting goals for themselves often make higher demands for themselves than their superiors and methods engineers consider to be practical. A furnace-cleaning job was cut from four to two days . . . service calls were reduced from one in fourteen to one in twenty-one . . . repairs per man per day rose from 8.5 to 12.5 when the crew planned the service. [2.3]

As some companies have demonstrated, it is possible to take production through the roof simply by organising participative meetings and harnessing the abundance of *managerial* competence that exists at lower levels. This can be done by asking employees to sort out problems for themselves and to make their own decisions. Use of this method can make tremendous thrusts of expertise available to the company. And it is also a popular method, for what employees want most of all is to become the masters of their working environment. An industrial psychologist has found that groups of factory workers having instructions carefully explained to them did not significantly increase their output. Those who had both an explanation *and* a chance to decide how to act on the instructions increased their output considerably. No doubt participative methods are easier to introduce in relatively new companies where patterns of power and influence are not deeply engrained.

## Braking forces

A powerful braking force on the trend towards decision-sharing is the undemocratic nature of most companies. The votes that control them go to money not people; the running is done by a small and powerful group (the board); power rests at the apex.

Already in Britain company law is being restyled so as to bring the employees' voice into the board rooms. And many think that such a change is overdue, for times have changed and workers have changed. Employees are better educated, more sophisticated than they were a few decades ago, and they are better equipped to contribute to company plans and policy. No doubt the future will see far more joint meetings of managers and employees, called to discuss manpower requirements, delivery dates, new machinery and other matters once considered the exclusive concern of management.

Managers themselves often resist decision-sharing. According to an industrial psychologist, M.H. Knowles, it is the neurotic, authoritarian personality who often gets himself promoted to managerial position; and organisations are full of emotionally unstable executives who can neither express their own feelings nor listen properly to other people's.

Other authorities argue that managers have unconscious aggressive feelings and lust for power that drastically limit their ability, say, to meet trade union representatives and negotiate with them rationally and on equal terms — although, admittedly, many unions seem to be better at fighting management than at cooperating with it to achieve joint goals.

## Dealing with the unions

One clue about how to deal with awkward union branches and representatives comes from Thrasher's work with delinquent teenage gangs. Thrasher found that the best way to influence these gangs was through their leaders. By concentrating attention on the leader and showing him ways of achieving status and security — the main motives for gang membership — by other means than the gang, Thrasher was able to change the attitude of the whole gang. For the rest followed the leader's example.

Perhaps, after all, the best way to deal with the militant shop steward or unofficial leader, is not to try to isolate him, not to seek less contact with him, but to seek more contact with him; to bring him onto work committees; to give him special responsibilities — such as chairing a group session or a departmental meeting. In this way the man — and his followers — might become involved in management purposes.

Indeed, involvement could be carried a stage further. The local union branch could be invited to accept more responsibility for discipline or working conditions — length and times of tea-breaks, holiday arrangements, and so on. Having to take executive action of this kind would surely sharpen the union's awareness of management's problems and stimulate a greater sense of responsibility. And so, in this way, the union could be groomed to play a more positive role.

James Burnham has stated:

'Experience has proved that trade unions are not an anti-capitalist institution; not subversive of capitalist control over the instruments of production to any important or long-term extent, but are precisely capitalist institutions organised on the basis of, and presupposing capitalist economic relations.' [2.4]

Arguably, the greatest communication barrier in industry is that between management and the workers. Often these two groups misunderstand and mistrust each other because of different goals, backgrounds and responsibilities. But these barriers *can* be overcome — not least by both sides agreeing to sit round the same table and talk about common problems.

Many managers still jib at the thought of introducing wide-ranging consultative processes, fearing that this would mean relinquishing some of their powers. Perhaps they are right. Perhaps each extra decision-sharing meeting or consultative committee that they set up represents a real transfer of authority. But perhaps, too, the most formidable communication barriers in modern industry can only be overcome by this kind of radical transformation.

When people from both sides of industry sit around the same table they begin to understand one another's viewpoint. Employees leave the meetings with a better understanding of management's problems. Management gains the information and feedback that it needs for sound decisions and, perhaps, is able to spot labour grievances before they become critical. Moreover, by tapping the employees' know-how in these meetings, management may be able to find ways of cutting operating and production costs.

Small, informal get-togethers, in particular, are useful because everybody can have his say without being overawed by the size and formality of the meeting.

Joint meetings can heal the cleavage in social ethics between managers and workers. For instance, the problem of output restriction can be overcome by *(a)* calling the employees into a meeting then *(b)*giving them the chance to *talk themselves* into a change of attitude.

In the group sessions organised by such firms as Polaroid and Parish Instruments, employees are invited to make decisions about production, purchasing and other problems, such as what kind of machinery to buy. Other firms call meetings at which employees set *their own* production goals — usually with good results.

These are just some of the reasons why, when the two sides of industry are far apart, meetings can be effective bridge-builders.

*Management meetings are an essential device for exchanging information and coordinating functions. They bring together people from different levels of management and from different parts of the organisation, and ensu.e that they cooperate in achieving corporate goals. Meetings of this kind improve relationships between people who, at all other times, are separated by physical and psychological space. Just as important, they put pressure on individual managers and experts to account for their work — and to improve their results.*

# 3
# Management meetings

Management meetings take time and money. But they are cheaper and quicker than squirming round the roadblocks that otherwise get thrown up between different parts of the organisation.

Basically there are only five or six reasons for holding meetings*:
—to coordinate and control
—to inform, or collect information
—to negotiate
—to consult
—to solve problems and make decisions
—to plan

Perhaps the last item on the list has no right to be there. So many companies seem to run blindly into avoidable disasters in spite of the best efforts of their planning committees. (Dunlop's plan was a

---

* Sir Kenneth Wheare [3.1] distinguishes six types of committee: committees to advise, to inquire, to negotiate, to legislate, to administer, and to scrutinise and control.

prelude to several years of depressed profits, huge losses on rubber futures, and the Pirelli merger fiasco.)

Low-level meetings tend to be informational in aim while high-level meetings tend more to problem-solving and decision-making. The most sensitive information about company affairs typically reaches the manager during a meeting (formal or informal) — perhaps because face-to-face communication is faster and more accurate than writing, and it is easier to ensure confidentiality.

According to one survey there is no uniform pattern of meetings in companies — a view that most of us would support from our own observation. Some companies have an elaborate network of meetings as a contribution to collective management. Others hold meetings only on an *ad hoc* basis to sort out unusual problems or sudden crises. Nevertheless, several investigators have discerned definite trends:

1    *Generally, there are more informal meetings and fewer formal*

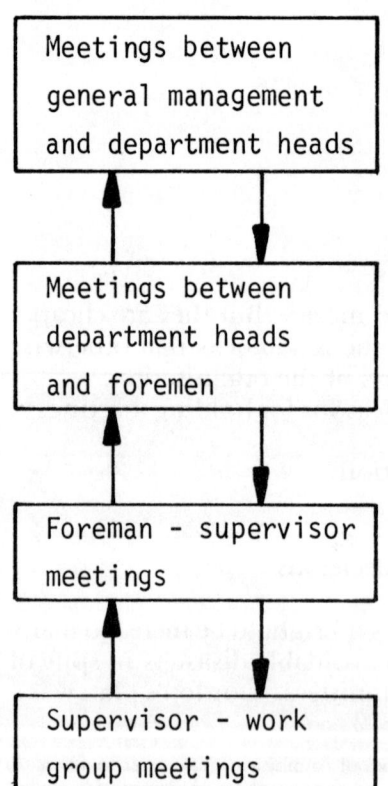

**Figure 2**   *Some companies communicate with the work force by a chain of small meetings. These can be called at short notice and used to pass information up or down the line with a minimum of distortion*

*committees than in the past* [3.2]. Thus one manager reported: 'Twice a year we have meetings with all our branch managers to introduce our new lines. We also have quarterly meetings with our area managers. There are no other formal meetings. The directors are in constant discussion . . . we just get together at the big table over there.' Another executive reports: 'Lots of my meetings are informal in the evenings with my executives . . . The working day is too valuable to be tied up in long meetings.' One company holds formal management meetings only about four times a year, yet has daily informal lunch meetings for executives.

2   *There are more* ad hoc *meetings and fewer standing committees than in the past* [3.3].

3   *Large firms hold more meetings than small firms* — presumably because teamwork is needed to solve the many problems of coordination and control faced by large companies. In very small companies, the boss should be able to coordinate all activities in his own mind. One firm I know which has 60 employees held only three management meetings in six months — and they were held only to allay rumours.

4   *Committee meetings become more important and more frequent at the higher levels of management.* Generally, senior managers serve on more committees than junior or middle managers [3.4].

## Kinds of committee

Practice varies considerably. But according to Copeman, Holden and his colleagues, and other authorities, the kinds of committee most commonly set up in companies include the following:

1   *Staff meetings*, called by department heads to discuss operating problems and to give the latest news about new recruits, new products, and so on. They are also useful for briefing staff on wider issues. At Honeywell, for instance, there are regular sessions on 'the corporate environment' to show people in the departments where the whole organisation is heading. Managers at these meetings also pass on information that they picked up at other meetings, on business trips, etc.

An important secondary aim of staff meetings is to build group identity and to get staff involved in running the department. So why not ask staff what *they* would like to discuss? Ask them to report on their work so that you learn what is happening in your own department.

Some managers use these sessions for giving instructions to staff: several studies have shown that employees generally prefer to receive instructions orally because of opportunities for feedback and clarification. Allow adequate time for questions and discussion at the end. And where the instructions are complicated, why not follow up the meeting with a memo repeating the main points and detailing the specific tasks required of particular people?

Staff meetings are most effective when they are held at two or three-week intervals: if they are held too often this creates apathy for the same ground is covered again and again; if too seldom, news becomes stale and the agenda is invariably over-crowded. Only two levels should attend briefing sessions — the department head and his immediate subordinates. If several levels attend there is the danger of weakening the immediate subordinates' authority because of by-passing.

2   *Budget meetings* (or meetings with a different name but similar purpose), whose function is to allocate scarce resources — money, materials and men — to competing uses. Typically, budget meetings *(a)* approve operating and capital expenditure, *(b)* supervise the actual spending, *(c)* monitor the results, so that problems are spotted and dealt with as soon as they appear.

*Supervision of large-scale spending is essential: if people are simply left to get on with their jobs, very large sums of money may be spent on useless or unrewarding work before anybody notices.*

Budget meetings usually have the power to revise particular budgets upwards or downwards as necessary; and to put pressure on inefficient managers to improve their results.* Individual executives can discuss their problems — shortages of raw materials, manpower problems, etc. — with other executives and try to find solutions.

A strong case could be made out for holding budget meetings at several levels in some organisations: at top level to supervise large-scale spending that stretches several years into the future; and at lower levels to supervise small-scale, short-term spending. This would be consistent with the sound management principle of push-

---

* *Most* managers are inefficient according to one managing director who reckons that only 2 per cent of the population are 'natural' leaders, but that 10 per cent of those in industry have to be leaders. This leaves a gap of 8 per cent who wear the management badge without management ability to back it up.

ing work down to the lowest level competent to deal with it — which means getting the job done as cheaply as possible.

3 *Project or product meetings* keep key people involved in a product or project up to date with progress. Planners and implementers, theoretical and practical people, e.g. R & D, Production, Marketing or Manufacturing, can explain their problems and activities to each other, thus improving coordination.

Typically, these meetings approve new projects/products and monitor the progress of existing ones. Problems such as delays, overspending, manpower problems and the like, can be tackled by the entire project team as they arise.

Usually, meetings open with a quick survey of each line of activity, then go on to discuss major problems. If meetings are held less frequently than every two or three weeks, problems build up and half the time can be spent reminding people what was covered in the last meeting.

Brief reports of the main points raised in each meeting can form a useful record of progress, and can also be used to show any actions required by individuals.

4 *Research and development meetings.* In most industries, the R & D effort requires large-scale financial, operational and administrative support, so that a coordinating committee is essential. Various staff specialists and the R & D team can come together in meetings to agree on areas where research is needed and to monitor the existing programme. Sometimes the sales, marketing and financial executives need to remind the R & D men that the basic reason for being in business is not to produce the fanciest hardware but the most profitable. And when funds are demanded for a project the committee may need to ask how the proposers know that the new product will eventually sell, and how soon it will pay off.

The need for the committee itself to exercise financial control instead of relying on the accountants and auditors, is pointed up by the comments of one financial director:

> We do an awful lot of R & D. But I don't recall that our auditors look at any but the most expensive projects. There is never any follow-up to see if the company actually ends up with the patents that should follow the research.

One economist has pointed to the great number of 'technically inappropriate' R & D projects in the United States. 'Even up to recent times', he comments, 'according to American research data, from 60 to 90 per cent of such corporate projects turned out to be either inappropriate or completely ineffectual' [3.5].

5   *Management councils* (or some similar name). Aim: to transmit information about new plans and policies to the rest of the organisation. Thus the membership is often large and drawn from several levels. Typically, meetings consist of reports by department heads on activities in their departments. This is sometimes followed by a report by a director on the last board meeting. In one company, the management council has 23 members from different levels of management. It meets weekly and hears reports about the current activities of the product divisions.

6   *Executive committees* are the highest organ in many large companies in Europe and the United States. Even Du Pont's vast empire is run by a small executive committee. This eight-man body is also the model for General Motors and many other companies. Each member is a senior vice-president charged with keeping the committee advised on everything going on in two to five of the company's twenty-five departments.

On most executive committees the members are senior managers and at least some of them are usually board members too. Typically, the executive committee (or whatever it calls itself) meets once or twice a week to review the operations of the whole company and to take decisions on planning, production and other major policy matters.

## The board of directors

Every company has at least one formal committee — the board of directors. This, in theory, is responsible for the whole organisation and has power to approve basic policies, declare dividends and approve capital expenditure.

In practice, the roles played by boards of different companies vary widely. Some are mere rubber stamps, endorsing decisions and programmes already made by committees or senior managers. Others act more like policemen, constantly checking on managerial actions, and revising policy from time to time. Some people argue that monitoring the performance of the chief executive — and replacing him if necessary — is the director's main function.

(Though if a company need a board to manage it, perhaps it needs new managers.)

Often boards set up committees such as executive, financial, audit, investment and salary committees. According to Ralph Lewis, the most effective board committees comprise 'three to five members who take their jobs seriously and submit written reports to their board well in advance of the board meetings at which their subjects are to be discussed' [3.6].

Most boards meet once a month. A few companies alternate the meeting place between headquarters and factories so that directors can see and be seen by local managers.

According to Holden and his colleagues (in *Top Management*), boards are typically 15 strong with about 60 per cent of the members drawn from outside the company. But there is some evidence that the most efficient companies are headed by very small boards:

> The companies which most frequently used capital effectively were headed by a board of about five directors and had a turn-over of about £1—3 million. [3.7]

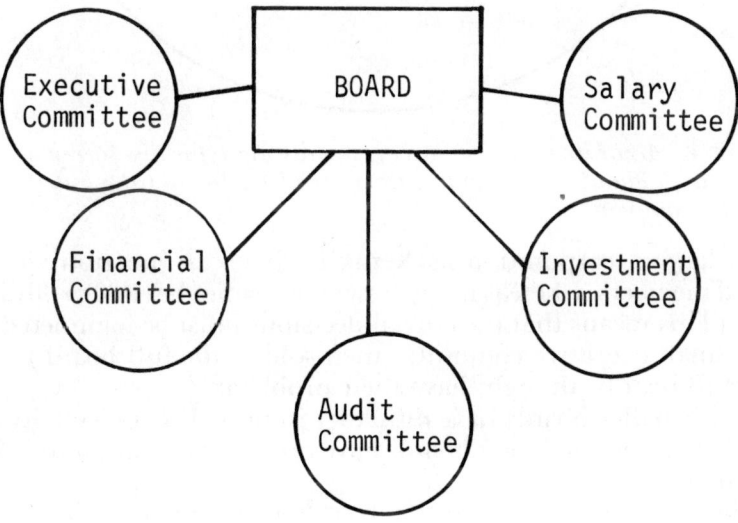

**Figure 3**   *The boards of most large companies set up committees to help them with policy-making. The most common board committees are those shown here. Typically, they consist of three to five members and submit written reports to their board before the board meeting at which their subjects are discussed*

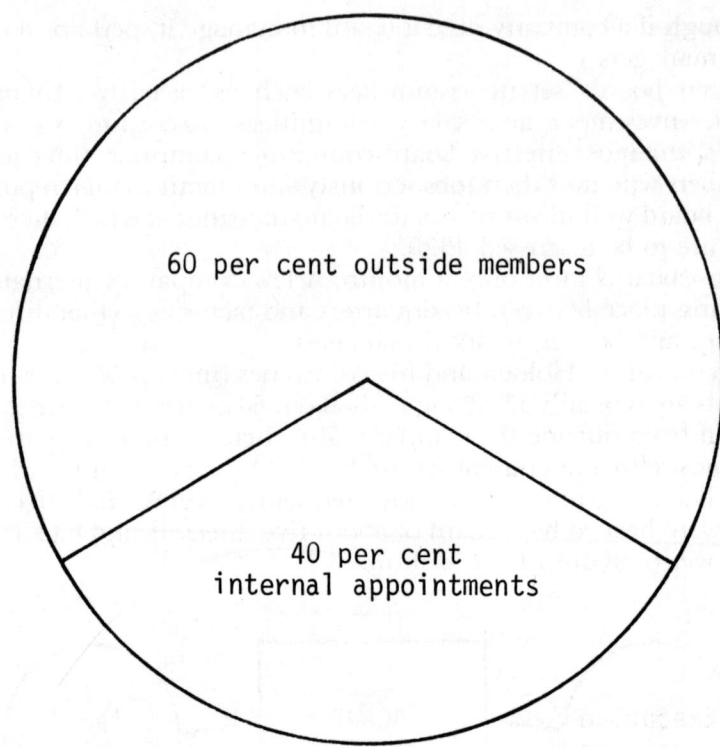

60 per cent outside members

40 per cent
internal appointments

**Figure 4**   *According to one survey, boards are typically fifteen strong with about 60 per cent of their members drawn from outside the company*

As large a corporation as Xerox finds it can function with 13 board members, whereas many lesser companies have 20 or 30 directors. (This means that the crucial decisions must be hammered out by a small executive committee then sold to the full board.)

Small boards, though, have their problem:

> ... smaller boards have difficulty in providing objectivity and balance while larger boards have problems of communication. [3.8]

The same source suggests that boards tend to grow in size as their responsibilities increase: a board of three members is likely to be responsible for under 25 employees, while a board of nine or ten members is more likely to be responsible for between 500 and 1000 employees. Usually, a large board considers and decides major policy questions and allows a smaller executive committee to make interim decisions.

**Board members**

Board members seem to require *(a)* a real competence in some field, *(b)* diverse business connections and *(c)* an independent judgement. Perhaps the importance of the last two qualities explains why so many board members are recruited from outside the company. A report written in 1973 for the Conference Board and the American Society of Corporate Executives, and drawing conclusions from a survey of 855 companies, showed that 71 per cent of *manufacturing* companies have a majority of outsiders on their boards and 86 per cent of non-manufacturing companies.

According to Ralph Lewis, a board member requires:

> analytical intelligence; the capacity to evaluate strategy; awareness of the social, political and economic environment; the ability to size up the CEO's chief subordinates; and an understanding of the company's strengths and weaknesses. [3.9]

When managers from inside the company are brought onto the board they may take their own specialised views into board meetings and shrug off the larger problems of the company as irrelevant or incomprehensible. Yet they are brought onto the board not to press their own particular, departmental interests but to contribute to *general* policy — and to present to the board essential information in layman's language. A way of helping departmental managers to gain the over-all view is for the board to give them general assignments, such as corporate planning activities, or projects which require close liaison with senior board members.

But in the long term, the best preparation for board responsibilities and general management may well be the kind that Lord Robens practised when he was head of the Coal Board in Britain, which involved a planned rotation through several departments before elevation to general management.

But without this kind of training, the double-role played by department heads who are promoted to the board, means that many 'have a real difficulty in keeping their two identities separate in their minds: it is a compelling argument for sending potential boardroom candidates on administrative courses at an early stage in their careers' [3.10]. Perhaps a case could be made out for sending *all* managers who are members of top-level committees on administrative courses, to wrench them out of the specialist or departmental approach to overall company problems.

## Image-building

Clearly, the careful selection of members is essential if a board is to have sufficient perspective for setting sound *strategic* goals — rather than merely reacting to events in a tactical way. Yet there is evidence to suggest that few boards commit themselves to systematic goal-setting, despite all the risks that *ad-hocracy* entails:

> Those companies that could not agree as to corporate direction could not define responsibility for decision-making, nor were likely to identify changes in the trading environment. [3.11]

Some boards seem to be very remote bodies — an impression created largely by their published accounts, reports, and the other goods they choose to display in the company shop-windows. Many boards could improve their image by making their annual reports plainer in language, sprightlier in presentation and easier to understand by the people who matter — the shareholders and the public.

One reason for the stale and stuffy flavour of many annual reports is that they are usually published only after the auditors have crawled all over them. This makes for reliable but dull reading because most of the facts and figures are already out of date.

Why don't more companies publish a preliminary report, *before* inspection by the auditors (to be followed by the usual, dreary, authorised version several months later)? This could highlight the kind of information that the public finds most interesting: forecasts of sales, product by product; earnings by specific products or divisions; the state of the market; and so on. And all because the public has a *right* to know.*

## Inter-departmental meetings

Organisations are like kaleidoscopes. You look through the eye-piece and if you're an accountant you see a financial problem, if you're the sales director you see a sales problem, and so on. In one investigation 23 managers were given a case history of a company to study; 83 per cent of the sales executives identified the major problem of the company as a sales problem, 80 per cent of the production managers saw a production problem, and so on. What each man sees as the facts of the case depends on his position in the organisa-

---

* Perhaps the public also have a right to know how the *government* is doing, department by department, year by year. Perhaps the government too should be producing easily digestible annual reports — for presentation to the tax-payers. After all, the government, like a company, is in the business of managing people and resources.

tion. He is securely locked inside a role — unless he is wrenched out of it by regular exposure to very different viewpoints, for instance, in inter-departmental meetings, where the following kind of exchange is likely to take place:

*Quality Control:* I want the best components available.

*Finance:* Get the cheapest.

*Production:* Get the quickest.

At this point, each man is forced to take stock of the other men's demands.

A group of psychologists, sociologists and other specialists attend a ten-week symposium. They begin by trying to agree on a definition of 'organisation'. Ten weeks later they are still trying. No two specialists can agree.

People from different disciplines and different departments see skewed pictures of reality. But managers in all departments need clear vision. This explains the value of inter-departmental meetings, for they are a way of pulling all the separate facets together and achieving an over-view. That is why, at General Motors, there used to be regular meetings between divisional heads — Buick, Cadillac, etc. — and the four-man executive committee. The idea was to test out new *ideas* on the practical men and thus lessen the danger of a separation between long-term planning and day-to-day operations. Part of the purpose of these meetings was 'to lift the eyes of the divisions from the floors of their factories up to the horizon, and see where the whole enterprise ought to be heading' [3.12].

### Better understanding between departments

A policy committee was set up in a large construction company with two members appointed from each department. Thus the departments (through their representetives) were making company policy. Conversely, policy was being relayed direct to the departments for discussion as soon as it was made. In this company, departments *acted* — not merely reacted — with regard to corporate policy. Every department gained a clear knowledge of company goals and of how all the departments, in different ways, were helping to achieve them. And as a result of the meetings, understanding between the departments improved.

In another company, inter-departmental meetings were used to launch an MBO system: departments were invited to meet and ham-

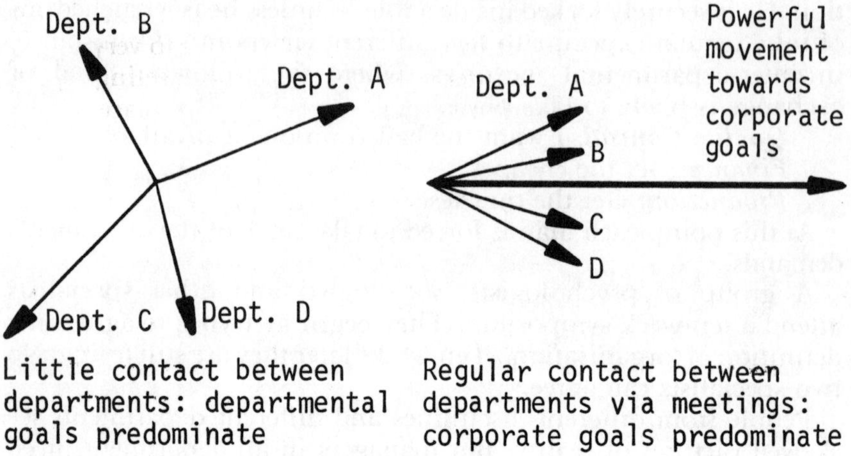

Dept. B

Dept. A        Dept. A          Powerful
                                movement
                                towards
                         B      corporate
                                goals

                         C
                         D

Dept. C    Dept. D

Little contact between        Regular contact between
departments: departmental     departments via meetings:
goals predominate             corporate goals predominate

**Figure 5** *Frequent inter-departmental meetings help to ensure that all departments move in the same direction, i.e. towards corporate goals*

mer out the *corporate* master-plan; then, by referring to this blueprint, to devise *departmental* goals.

Think of the range and variety of ideas that can be brought to bear on company problems when people from different departments sit round the same table. The enticing possibilities prompt one company to hold weekly meetings of department heads to review the sales figures. The meetings provide guidelines for each department's activities in the following week: each meeting produces an action set of minutes with the department that is required to take action named in the margin.

A strong case could be made out for allowing managers from other parts of the organisation to attend meetings in your own department and even share in the decision-making. For major decisions taken by the department will probably affect all the others. For instance, a decision about labour relations or advertising policy will affect the basic demand and supply pattern in the company which, in turn, affects each department.

If managers from other departments attended meetings in your own department they could perform a staff or consultancy function by giving advice in the areas of their special competence.

## Curbing the empire-builders

All large organisations have severe problems of coordination and control. Patterns of communication tend to be complex. Blockages occur at numerous junctures — despite the advantages of free access. As the organisation grows and becomes more complex its parts interlock more completely. Changes in one department have an impact on all the others.

Thus constant contact between departments is needed to make sure that their activities harmonise. Otherwise, they find themselves working towards contradictory goals with each department seeing its own function in isolation from the wider organisations: each department feels that group loyalty means grabbing the biggest possible share of resources.

Fortunately, frequent inter-departmental meetings can build bridges and wrench departments out of their isolationism. Head-collectors and empire-builders (who equate power and possessions with effectiveness) are forced to modify their demands when they are sitting opposite managers from other departments who have equal claims on the same slender funds. As a result, there is a gradual shift in emphasis within each department from *possessions* to *performance* as the yardstick of effectiveness.

## Informal links — then meetings

Rice has described an inter-departmental meeting in a textile mill where relations between the participants were strained:

> ... divisional managers did not appear to communicate very much with each other ... they spent a large part of the time at the management meetings I attended in attacking each other and defending themselves from attack. Criticism of policy and plans tended to be more destructive than constructive. [3.13]

How much value for money was the company getting from those meetings? Surely, when relations between departments and divisions are as strained as they seemed to be in the textile mill, a lot of preparatory spadework is needed before a formal meeting is held. Otherwise, the meeting itself will only exacerbate an already tense situation.

When relations between departments are poor, why not lead up to an inter-departmental meeting gradually. For instance, you could invite managers from the other departments to have coffee in your office occasionally. Or you could do the necessary footwork and go and talk shop to managers in their own departments. Gradually a sympathetic understanding will be built up between at least some of the managers in the different departments — and at this stage you could suggest holding a meeting.

## Meetings between different levels and disciplines

Meetings between different specialists and different levels can also bring together people who are poles apart in their thinking. Mutual understanding and cooperation grows as they are exposed, in meetings, to each other's problems and ideas. Direct contact injects warmth and precision into future communication between them. This is the thinking at Matsushita where divisional heads spend no more than an hour or two a day at their desks: the rest of the time is spent in formal and informal discussion with managers from different levels and different divisions.

Meetings attended by different levels of management can improve relationships and boost productivity. Rice reports a meeting of this kind in *The Enterprise and its Environment*. The supervisor in charge of a weaving shed called the meetings, but they were attended by the chairman, the general manager, the works manager, charge hands and operatives — in fact, the whole executive chain responsible for production. Work problems were frankly discussed and grievances ironed out. As a result, relationships between the different levels improved. After a slow start, general efficiency in the shed increased, and with it the quality of cloth, until both were higher than in the other sheds where meetings of this kind were not held.

Multi-level meetings allow direct communication between senior and junior people. How many technical improvements and innovations could spring from this kind of contact? (One investigator surveyed managers in 31 food and electronics factories, and concluded that the more channels linking top and bottom levels the more chance that new ideas and undistorted feedback will be transmitted to decision-making levels, thus leading to necessary changes and innovations.)

Multi-level meetings are particularly useful for passing information about company affairs to the entire organisation. All levels get the same information at the same time and in the same words — thus avoiding the kind of distortion that happens when messages are sent down the chain.

*Use meetings to check the relevance of work by the back-room boys*

## Wasting money

Meetings of this kind are ways of checking on the activities of technical specialists, many of whom become so enamoured with their own pet projects that they lose sight of making money. I once knew an OR man who worked for a full year on an impossibly complex forecasting system. Everybody in his section knew that he was riding a sure loser. But the OR man didn't know this. So he carried on happily playing his crazy maths game and doing his computer runs — simply because he was never required to explain the relevance and usefulness of his work to a group of other specialists in a meeting.

During meetings which bring together different specialists, specific operating problems can be discussed and critical decisions taken by the entire team which is involved in a product or project.

*Project and product meetings* bring together specialists from many different disciplines. Each man can find out, by direct contact, about the problems and responsibilities of other experts who are involved in the project. He can also check that his own problems and responsibilities are understood by everybody else.

The success of meetings of this kind depends largely on the choice of chairman. He needs to be an impartial senior manager — the chairman of an inter-departmental meeting should come from a department which is not represented at the meeting; the chairman of a meeting of experts should ideally be a non-technical generalist, and so on. He should have skill in dealing with people and the sort of objective approach that allows him to keep out of the doctrinal storms. For meetings between different specialists can be very tense and very prejudiced affairs. One reason is that experts often develop a strong emotional attachment to a particular scheme or a pet idea and just won't let go of it:

> . . . the emotional involvements tend to block understanding. Since the men did not tend to deal with emotions their inhibiting effects were never explored. On the contrary, *they were covered up by the use of technical, rational arguments.* [3.14] *(My italics.)*

In meetings between specialists, 'rational' arguments are often no more than irrational feelings thinly disguised with technical jargon. Usually, the disguise is so thin that others quickly spot the weaknesses in the argument and launch counter-attacks.

## Each meeting a magnet

An ILO report on industrial communication points out that the more complex the organisation the more detailed are the steps which management must take to ensure that information reaches all parts of the organisation, and that information from all parts is fed back to itself. This is one of the reasons why complex organisations need good formal systems of communication such as committees, meetings of the kind described above, and other tools for welding the component parts of the monster into a single living organism.

Each meeting should be a magnet that draws managers out of their departments or specialists out of their laboratories and gets them round the same table discussing common problems and how to consolidate their efforts to achieve company goals.

*Many managers use meetings not as democratic devices (the official reason), but in the interests of orderly government. For instance, a senior manager may allow a committee to put in the long hours of discussion and analysis of a problem — then take the decision himself. Many managers use meetings to sell their ideas to their colleagues, or to put pressure on their staff to improve their performance, or for image-building purposes. Sometimes, a clique of managers wins control of the most important committees in the organisation and so gets a strangle-hold on decision-making. When this happens, the organisation needs to act quickly to penalise these men.*

# 4
# Managers' motives

When General Eisenhower marched into the White House he is reputed to have taken the army 'staff system' with him. Each Cabinet member was given complete authority in his own area, which enabled him to act with military efficiency and decision. But when a problem overlapped two or more departments, or when it was an exceptionally tough and complicated problem, the President would set up an *ad hoc* committee to handle it.

Like many top-level executives, Eisenhower was adept at using meetings and committees to strengthen his own executive control. According to Richard Nixon, he deliberately *used* meetings as devices for focusing the combined brain-power of the White House on Presidential problems [4.1]. These meetings did the spadework, put in the long hours of analysis and argument. But once they had drawn up their reports or made their recommendations, the President made sure that it was he alone who took the decision.

Eisenhower acted in the best managerial manner. Many senior

managers use meetings in precisely this way: not in the interests of democracy but in the interests of orderly government.

Who can blame them? Does any manager feel happy about accepting somebody else's decision when the manager himself will have to answer for it? (On the other hand, managers have to do precisely that if they want their subordinates to grow in commitment and responsibility.) That is why command meetings, i.e. meetings called by a senior manager and attended by his staff, are run in the way that they are. Whatever the procedure used in the meeting, the manager who calls it is really making the decision. If the manager accepts the majority view then his acceptance automatically makes the decisions his own. For, as Wilfred Brown has explained, management philosophy is that the person held accountable for a decision should be the one who makes it.

*Officially, meetings are devices for power-sharing, for exchanging information, for coordinating functions. But unofficially, managers can use them for quite different ends — to strengthen their own control and power in the organisation.*

## More meetings — more control

One manager told me that he sees meetings simply as an opportunity for leaning heavily on his staff and making them think clearly about their jobs. Another manager said, 'Frankly, I use meetings as a kind of sounding-board for thinking my problems out loud. I never feel bound by their recommendations.'

John deButts, Chairman of American Telephone and Telegraph, sees meetings as an administrative tool for tightening his own control over that vast corporation — and therefore for boosting his own power and influence:

> When I first came to this job, I decided I wanted strong rapport with the managements of all our telephone companies . . . So I set myself the task of visiting all the companies and talking to their management groups . . . . I wanted them to know what my objectives were and the direction in which I wanted this business to go. And I wanted to get an idea from them as to what things were worrying them . . . . I started with a short, formal presentation to the management. Then I spent a loose, unstructured period with the president and his people . . . . Frequently the best time to meet the people in our subsidiaries is when they are already going to have a meeting any-

way . . . This sort of thing is worth the time to me because it keeps me in touch; *it lets me check the formal reports I receive against the realities.* [4.2] *(My italics.)*

He claims that when confronted by an important issue he listens carefully to what his senior executives think — then takes the decision himself.

Most ambitious executives, I am convinced, use meetings not as a device for power-sharing, but as a weapon for attaining their own ends. They *use* meetings to sell proposals or to justify decisions they have already taken; or to win people's cooperation in putting those decisions into effect. To many managers, meetings are an opportunity to pick up helpful hints about what is going on in the organisation, what new alliances are forming, whose knives are out and where the corpses are hidden. Who can blame managers for asking themselves in meetings: How will this decision affect me and my department? Will it help us or will it hurt us? Is it the kind of decision I wish to push or to block? How dangerous would it be to block the proposal?

Meetings present department heads with an opportunity to apply crude but salutary pressure on their staffs to produce good results and keep them thinking about their jobs. One manager told Copeman: 'I have a monthly budget meeting . . . why aren't sales targets being met . . . why are expenses over their budgets . . . I don't worry about the figures that are on-target' [4.3].

*Meetings put pressure on managers to get better results*

Meetings by exception are also the rule in the John Walter Corporation. The operating units in this billion-dollar group are given a completely free reign — until something goes wrong. At that point, headquarters calls a meeting. The facts are placed on the table. The autopsy begins. After one such meeting, a plant manager who had just had to swallow some rather strong and nasty medicine asked the chairman of the company when he could expect to see him again. The laconic reply was, 'You have two bad months and you'll see me again'.

## Black mist

Because they are clever enough and careful enough, some autocratic managers manage to rule their departments by means of 'democratic' meetings.

Worker participation may be in vogue. But managers still have to manage, still have to think in terms of control, power and performance. Because without power and authority there can be no discipline and ultimately no survival. Robert McMurry, an American business consultant, has pointed out that 'an executive without power is all too often a figurehead — or worse, headless'.

Often an individual executive isn't 'heavy' enough — or fly enough — to push a decision through on his own. So he has recourse to the Plural Executive — a clique of managers conspiring to achieve common goals. Thus the decision-maker's greatest asset is friends in high places.

The pursuit of power involves alliances at all levels. These are formed in numerous formal and informal meetings; and at pre- and post-meeting confabs where common goals and tactics are agreed and common enemies identified. (I was present at one furtive session when an offer of support in a particular meeting was traded in return for a promise of a particular organisational change.) This kind of wheeling-dealing and influence-peddling is what the Japanese call the 'black-mist', and it swirls round the executive corridors of every large company. How many corporate decisions are spun out of it?

*Through its murky influence, many a managerial clique has got a stranglehold on decision-making — in effect, won control of the important committees — and so made sure that any proposals that don't fit in with their own plans are quickly and quietly aborted.*

Sometimes meetings are used in more subtle ways. For instance,

*Often proposals that fail to fit in with top managers'
plans are quietly strangled*

one manager I know uses them to *stop* decisions being made. To
stop a particular proposal going through, he calls a meeting and
takes the chair himself. He is an experienced chairman and he runs
the meeting in such a way that the discussion goes on and on, back-
wards and forwards, without an agreement being reached. But everybody does agree when the chairman suggests that, in the absence of
any agreement, the proposal should be shelved!

## Gallery of fronts

For the ambitious executive meetings are

a stage for exploratory skirmishes; for making authoritative
hints to those moving too far in some direction; for the study of
faces and inflections; for catching slips and checking on pre-
meeting tips etc. The formal meeting is a gallery of fronts
where aimless, deviant and actual currents of action merge for a
moment.... All depart with new knowledge to pursue var-
iously altered but rarely the agreed, courses. [4.4]

The higher a manager climbs in his organisation the more likely
he is to use meetings for somewhat devious purposes like these,
because top managers who *don't* think constantly in terms of power
and influence don't stay at the top. Moreover, manipulating meetings, or the people who attend them, must be reckoned to constitute

a major part of the senior manager's job: because the higher a manager gets the more meetings he attends, as several diary-studies have shown. Indeed, many top-level managers commonly serve on a dozen or more committees.

Sometimes managers use meetings to sharpen and strengthen their own ideas — in effect, to improve the quality of the decisions that they alone will take. Pelz found that optimum performance is associated with *(a)* consulting some colleagues whose orientation differs from one's own — who challenge one's ideas and point out shortcomings; and *(b)* consulting some colleagues who share one's orientation — who support and develop one's ideas [4.5]. In most meetings the manager has the benefit of both kinds of consultation — and better decision-making is the result.

Thus meetings can help even the die-hard autocrat — not least because they give him the information and the feedback that he needs for sound decision-making. Moreover, even when a manager calls a meeting simply to rubber-stamp a decision he has already taken, it gives him the opportunity to convince people that the decision is right and deserves support. After all, important decisions are extremely difficult to carry out properly in the absence of wide-spread support in the organisation. The autocrat might judge the success of a meeting by how quickly and easily he was able to sell his proposals to the other participants. And sometimes, if he is very clever, they may think that *they* are selling his proposals to *him.* Those who outmanoeuvre their colleagues in this way are usually able to rationalise their tactics to themselves by believing that it's all for the general good and that it's in the company's interests that their ideas and proposals should win.

I am convinced from my own experience that most important decisions are not resolved in the meeting but before it. The meeting organiser meets with the participants, either singly or in small groups, discusses what he plans to do and gets reactions. Thus he can check on his proposals and be certain that they are acceptable. If he senses wide opposition to a particular proposal he lets it die on the spot.

### Ego-trips

According to one survey, many managers deliberately use meetings to impress their bosses — and are themselves impressed when their bosses impress *their* bosses in meetings. (Many studies have shown that managers are often judged by their ability to exert influence upwards.) According to this survey, meetings are often used unofficially for the following purposes:

1   *Image-building*, e.g. the ideas man, the sound no-nonsense executive, the master tactician.
2   *To impress subordinates*, e.g. with one's democratic management style.
3   *To demonstrate leadership* — either through the simple fact of organising and chairing a meeting or by winning a decision.
4   *To demonstrate conspicuously* that things are happening in your own area of command.

Meetings are also used as a mechanism for pushing through the kind of controversial decision that the manager would have been unable or unwilling to take alone. For instance, a decision by an individual manager to get rid of somebody or to carve up a department headed by an incompetent subordinate could easily touch off a tempest of passion and politics from which the manager himself might emerge distraught, dishevelled and eating his words. But if the same manager takes his proposal to a committee and can persuade that body to make the decision, he doesn't have to worry too much about a possible backlash, because it is very difficult to enforce collective accountability against a committee: it's just not practicable to make a *dozen* heads roll!

**Psychological support**

A meeting may strengthen a manager's hand in other ways. For instance, executives acting alone are often unwilling to take what for the company would be quite attractive risks — perhaps because long exposure to control procedures tends to bias managers and administrators against any decisions which could lead to losses. Thus many exciting opportunities are lost to the company: they are screened out at an early stage in the decision-making process by over-cautious decision-makers. But in meetings even ultra-cautious managers come alive, widen their vision, support attractive if somewhat risky proposals — or even put them forward themselves. It's as if the meeting, with the diffused responsibility that it offers, had acted as a trip-wire to release reserves of energy and initiative.

It is easier to take some decisions when the responsibility is shared with others. Really big decisions, for instance, are psychologically difficult to take alone. Supporting evidence for this view comes from an authoritative source — Lord Cobbold, former Governor of the Bank of England. Cobbold told the Bank Rate Tribunal, set up after the sensational decision to raise the bank rate to 7 per cent in 1957:

> It is nice to be able to share one's responsibilities with one's colleagues . . . . I think it very much strengthens the position of the Governor and Deputy Governor in making these decisions for the world to know that they are made under the responsibility of such an experienced and unbiased body of first-class citizens.

Evidence like this adds substance to John Kenneth Galbraith's claim (in *The New Industrial State*) that large modern organisations are run by a *technostructure*, comprising everyone in the organisation who shares in the decision-making, and that the real achievements of these organisations depend on a massive coordination of the efforts of many people. *According to Galbraith, it is groups of people, in meetings, who define organisational goals and who ultimately determine the allocation of resources. By contrast, shareholders and directors have little say in these matters. Galbraith's view leaves little room for the individualist view of management — the manager as Hero.*

Sharing the problem takes the sting out of decision-making for the individual executive. And the organisation benefits from meetings too. For they curb the naked power of authority by making even powerful individuals answerable — to some extent — to others in the organisation. They prevent too much power concentrating in any one pair of hands by giving many people a direct interest in the major areas of corporate activity.

## Two levels

Meetings help the manager to manage — for instance, by giving him the information he needs for sound decision-making. By tossing the ball back and forth in a meeting a group can communicate information to the boss which no single person on a man-to-man basis dare do.

All meetings operate on two levels simultaneously. There is the level of what the meeting is about officially — a review of expenditure, problem-solving, or whatever. And there is the level of what the meeting is really about from the point of view of the motives of those attending.

The unofficial reasons why managers organise and attend meetings include:

1   To impress bosses and subordinates.
2   To demonstrate leadership, e.g. by organising and chairing the meeting.
3   To kill proposals that don't fit in with the individual manager's own plans.
4   To gain psychological support for big or harsh decisions.
5   To gain prestige (rubbing shoulders with the great).
6   To sell proposals and win cooperation in implementing them.
7   To increase control over the organisation; to put pressure on operating units and individuals to produce good results.

When faced with a particularly tough and complex problem, many senior executives set up an *ad hoc* committee to do all the preparatory work and put in the hours of detailed argument — before taking the decision themselves on the basis of the committee's recommendations.

## Ground rules

Is it realistic to blame executives for using meetings in the way they do and manipulating decisions for their own ends? To act with enlightened self-interest — or better still, self-disinterest — participants in meetings must be able to see how their decisions relate to over-all company strategy. But many decisions in meetings are taken in the *absence* of clear and consistent corporate policy (or at least, in the absence of any awareness of it).

When the company as a whole lacks a clear sense of direction, it is inevitable that some decisions in meetings will be taken on the basis of self-interest. At the same time, such decisions can be very damaging to the company. For instance, the political assassination of a rival's proposal may mean the loss to the company of a new product or a new marketing opportunity. Perhaps every company should make a conscious effort to ensure that all managers are clear about company policy, and that the decisions they make in meetings reflect this policy. Managers who openly exploit meetings to achieve their own private goals should be checked and, if necessary, disciplined. As Antony Jay remarks:

> By all means assume that any given manager is always working exclusively for the general good of the whole corporation; but construct the system so that he is penalised if he is not. [4.6]

Such stern action may be needed from time to time, because most managers become adept at using meetings and committees to boost their own power and influence and to strengthen their own executive control. Often a meeting is asked to do the spadework — to put in the long hours of analysis and discussion — but the manager himself takes the decision. A survey of 166 senior managers by Frank Heller, reported in *Managerial Decision-making*, shows that the most frequently used method of making decisions is for a manager to consult with subordinates and then to make the decision himself. (The survey also reveals that the more important a decision is, the more likely that it will be made by managerial diktat.)

Managers see meetings as opportunities for selling proposals or for winning cooperation; and for putting pressure on staff to produce good results. Moreover, sharing the decision can take the sting out of decision-making by providing psychological support for harsh decisions and reduce the chances of a backlash.

Meetings are also used for demonstrating leadership, for image-building, for impressing bosses and subordinates. And sometimes a clique of top-level managers conspire to win control of key committees and use meetings to ensure that any proposals that fail to fit in with their own plans are quietly strangled.

Managerial meetings operate at two levels, the official and the unofficial: how often are decisions taken in them because the unofficial motives predominate?

*For some committeemen prejudice or self-interest is the name of the game. Others solve problems in meetings on the basis of hunch or precedent. But today, committees don't have to solve problems in this way for rational methods of problem-solving are available. Now tools of prediction and control have been perfected. And there are new problem-solving techniques for use in meetings — such as those described here.*

# 5

# A committee-man's guide to problem-solving

One meeting called by President Kennedy was to decide whether or not to veto a measure by Congress to protect domestic sugar producers against foreign competition. The meeting opened with Dean Rusk explaining why the State Department favoured a veto. Then the Secretary of Agriculture explained why he supported Congress. At this stage, Kennedy looked undecided, then said he'd better get Hubert Humphrey's opinion (whose home state of Minnesota is a major sugar producer). Humphrey was quickly brought into the meeting by phone. His voice crackled over the wire. Finally Kennedy put the phone down, hesitated a moment, then said, 'I guess I'll let it go through.'

It's amazing how many problem-solving meetings are run in this casual way — even those called by top people and attended by the best brains. How many important corporate decisions are the result of what Sir David Kelly has described as 'casual unreasoning action by ordinary men in positions of extraordinary power'? The costs to industry of this kind of problem-solving are frightening to contemplate.

Many important decisions are taken long before the meeting that is supposed to make them — perhaps behind closed doors by some furtive cabal; or by two or three wheeling executives in the golf-club bar.

Another brake on rational problem-solving in meetings is self-interest. Assume that most of the participants in any problem-solving meeting have personal interests of one kind or another — and that these interests will probably influence the kind of decisions that are made. The Congressman or MP or County Councillor who belongs to a political party can't often afford to exercise his independent judgment during meetings. The civil servant with shares may not always choose to do so. In management meetings, the department head can't help but see things in a partial and lop-sided way. The systems analyst on the Projects Committee is bound to be strongly prejudiced in favour of certain proposals and against others even before the discussion begins.

In some meetings every participant is trying to influence the decision in a self-interested way. Some members may have a tacit understanding with a certain group or section that they will, at every opportunity, push the committee in a certain direction — like the laser expert on the R & D Committee or the militant trade unionist on the Works Council.

## Irrational problem-solving

These are just some of the reasons why problem-solving meetings may produce inadequate or inappropriate solutions. For much more is going on in meetings than the generation and assessment of two or three alternatives. Many irrational forces are at work. For instance, how often is a particular solution chosen because members feel it's the one they *ought* to choose? And in many meetings, self-interest is the name of the game — a game which may soon become more difficult to play on public committees in Britain because of legislation to force members to declare their financial interests.

*One way of improving problem-solving in the organisation is to bring these particular problems out into the open by talking about them in meetings — for instance, at the end of normal business — then deciding what to do about them.*

Today, problems no longer need to be solved irrationally, or on the basis of self-interest or precedent; for new tools of prediction and control (statistical analysis, operations research, etc.) are available which are capable of turning problem-solving into a precise science. The organisation no longer needs to respond to new problems as if they were crises which only faith, hope and intuition are capable of solving. Even if the members of a problem-solving committee don't themselves understand the new techniques there is usually somebody in the organisation who does — and who should be invited to join the committee forthwith. (Clearly, meetings dealing with such problems as company-wide stock control or forecasting or planning should include people with the relevant *quantitative* skills.)

The growing complexity of business problems has coincided with the development of technical tools for handling them — although the tools themselves may be ignored because of innumerate managers (many of whom learnt how to manage in the days when business problems were still thought out and fought out exclusively in *words*). Information, for instance, can be assembled and processed today on a scale never possible before. The computer can take the guesswork out of decisions by producing masses of information at the right time. Thus calling the systems analyst into a meeting to decide future product lines or marketing policy could save hours of lightweight speculation and lead to a far better solution.

## Solutions by computer

The computer department may be able to come to the aid of your meeting — but only if the participants ask the right sort of questions. For computers can only answer certain kinds of question.

The logical inference is that people who regularly attend problem-solving meetings need to be trained in basic computer technology. Even a brief crash course that details the strengths and weaknesses of this valuable resource and the kind of questions it likes, would be better than no training at all. Professor Ackoff has argued that before any management information system is installed, the managers and committees for whom it is intended should be trained to use and control it — rather than be controlled by it.

Equally, the members of computer departments would benefit

from training. A short course on how to assess the information needs of managers and meetings would be invaluable, and would, no doubt, lead to better information and therefore better solutions. As many companies have discovered, computer departments have to be *trained* to translate the results of their searches into the language of the executive, i.e. language that sets forth simply and clearly the values, effectiveness and costs of alternative courses of action.

One consultant advises clients who don't have a computer to set up information centres — an enlarged and highly organised version of central files — to help the problem-solvers. Several days before a problem-solving meeting the chairman of the meeting could ring the centre and explain the problem to be considered. The archivist is a man trained in the efficient *oral* reporting of information, so that hours or even minutes later he could phone back with helpful information. It's easy to see that such an approach would save a lot of time, energy and money, and also cut through all the red tape that often piles up between information givers and users.

## The importance of information

*Problem-solving has been defined as the process of converting information into action; and high quality information is the essential raw material from which good solutions emerge.* High quality information is accurate, clear, timely and relevant to the problem. When the information available to the problem solver has these characteristics important new breakthroughs can be made:

> The great astronomer, Johann Kepler, had very bad eyesight. As a consequence, he spent very little time observing the celestial bodies that were his major interest. Instead, he studied data accumulated by fellow astronomers, and noted that their observations revealed regularities in the changing character of the firmament. What happened to one star was closely correlated with the movement of another, or with the successive locations of the sun or moon. After lengthy examination of recurrent patterns in the data, Kepler announced his discovery of the solar system. [5.1]

The quality of information available to members of a problem-solving meeting depends partly on the efficiency of the organisation's MIS; and partly on the initiative and expertise of the executive who called the meeting. (Can he anticipate the kind of information that will be required and does he know where to obtain it?) On the other hand, the fact-finding may be too big a job for the meeting organiser: it may require specialised statistical training in certain cases.

When assembling information for a meeting you should have no difficulty in getting relevant facts provided that you ask the right questions and go to the people who can answer them, i.e. to the appropriate level and to the right experts. The knack required is to pinpoint the problem by asking the right questions, so that you get exactly the facts you require.

Many managers learn from experience which information sources are reliable and use these sources more than others to ensure that they receive high-quality information. Some managers create resentment among subordinates by using Roosevelt's technique of checking and balancing information from official sources against information from a number of unofficial sources. For instance, several subordinates may be set to work independently — and unknown to each other — to collect the same body of information. The results are then carefully compared. The manager gets an all-round look at the problem and spots any inconsistencies or contradictions, and this strengthens his hand in committee. Only the subordinates suffer, when they learn how they've been used.

It would be easy to condemn such methods as devious, but at least they ensure that adequate, reliable information is available for problem-solving. Remember that while inadequate control may weaken a firm, inadequate information may destroy it — as Rolls Royce discovered when misinformation about the costs of an engine plunged it into bankruptcy.

## Information shortage

Here are two easily recognisable symptoms of information shortage:

*1 Certain items on the agenda are over-discussed.* This is usually because members are uninformed about them and have to spend a lot of time probing for and providing basic information.

*2 Decisions are made in surprisingly broad terms.* Individual executives are left to work out the details — even the important ones. For instance, a committee spent a lot of time considering a rationalisa-

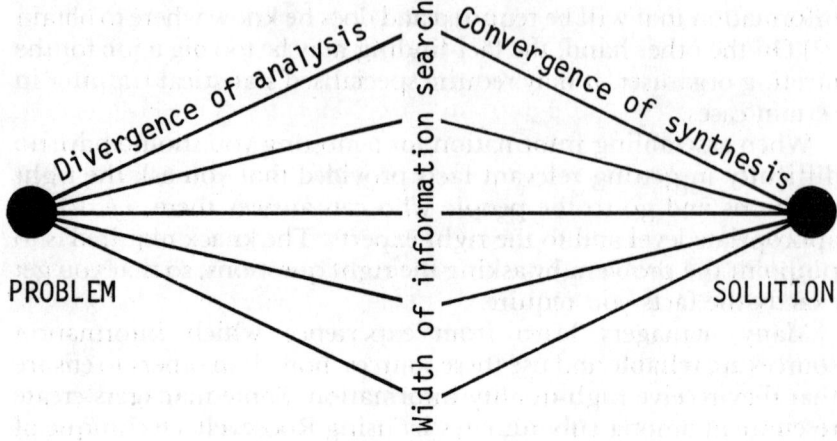

**Figure 6**   *Generally, the wider the information search the more focused and accurate the decision. But there are many risks involved in making wide searches, e.g. high costs, delays, the emergence of contradictory blocks of evidence and overloading of the members of the committee*

tion proposal. The end-product of all its deliberations was the bald recommendation that 'over the next twelve or eighteen months the labour force should be reduced by some 15-20 per cent'. No names, no dates, no ideas about how the run-down should be phased. Nothing about terms of compensation or how the scheme might be sold to the employees. All that was left to 'the administration', who thus acquired a responsibility they should never have had to carry.

*One way of improving the information service to committees is to ask senior managers to make a systematic study of the kind of problems dealt with by each major company committee.* This would allow its information needs to be identified. The central administration might then provide useful *general* information — sales figures, market trends and the like — on an occasional basis; and it would be better able to understand each committee's *specific* information needs when faced with any particular problem.

### How to confuse a committee

Some officials mistakenly assume that the more information they funnel to participants before a meeting the better their grasp of the problems will be. Just how mistaken this assumption can be is illustrated by the following case. Once I was a member of a committee that met fortnightly. A few days before each meeting a fat wad of 'working papers' would drop onto the hall floor. There were never fewer than a dozen closely typed sheets of information — of differing degrees of relevance and clarity — and sometimes quite a lot more.

The only way I could cope with this lot was to read the opening and closing paragraphs in full but the first sentence only of all the other paragraphs. In this way I managed to keep exhaustion and confusion at bay while getting some idea of the background to the problems.

The moral is clear: don't force committee members to read themselves to death just to find out what the problem is.

Too many undigested facts can change the problem-solver into a Hamlet paralysed by indecision. Moreover, the greater the bulk of information presented to members, the greater the chance that different blocks of it will imply *different* solutions. When this happens, the over-briefed and thoroughly confused committee has to fall back on precedent or hunch in formulating its solutions. (In any case, it is hardly ever possible to assemble enough information to remove *all* doubts about a decision.)

Another danger in providing over-abundant information before a meeting is that after studying it carefully, the members will — naturally enough — feel that they have fully understood the problem and so take up a 'position' and come to the meeting with their minds already made up. This can lead to inadequate or inappropriate solutions because if the problem had been as simple as that there would have been no need for a meeting in the first place.

Thus perhaps one of the basic tests of efficiency is *how little* information a committee needs to formulate good solutions. (It has been pointed out that human beings are conservative processors of information and don't extract from available information as much certainty as the evidence justifies.)

Of course, some meetings require more information than others — for instance, those dealing with complex technical problems. And some committees are temperamentally more cautious than others and demand more information as a basis for their decisions. High-risk decision-makers make their decisions as soon as they have enough information to indicate a fair chance of correctness. Conservative decision-makers wait until they have enough information to indicate a very good chance of correctness.

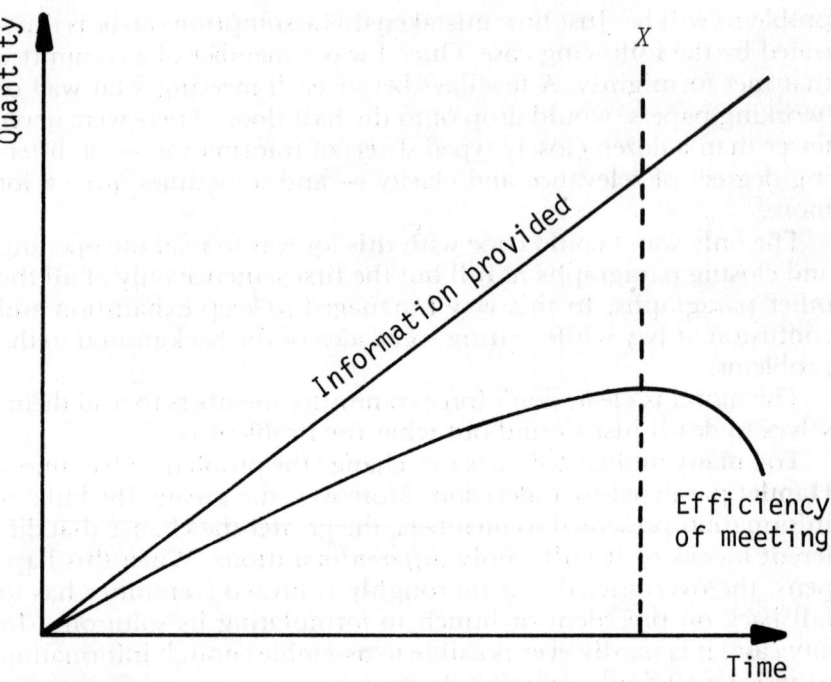

**Figure 7**  *Better decisions are made when high-quality information is available. But when too much information is provided members become confused and have to fall back on precedent or guesswork in making their decisions. For maximum value for money, stop the information search at point X — if you can identify it.*

### Briefing a committee

One manager told me that after calling a meeting he usually briefs himself by finding answers to the questions in this checklist:

1  What is official company policy on this problem?
2  What is the history of the problem?
3  What will be the impact of various solutions? (How will different operating units be affected?)
4  What will be the cost of implementing various solutions?
5  What does the managing director think?
6  What do the different departments think?

The answers to these questions help him to decide what preliminary information, if any, to send to the people who will be attending the meeting. Moreover, this careful self-briefing enables him to answer questions in the meeting and to keep up with the discussion in an intelligent way.

This manager reckons that working papers should be sent to the participants no more than three days before the meeting to ensure that the information is *up to date*. For in the can't-stop world of business the facts have a habit of changing from day to day. That is why a good method of ensuring that members are getting up-to-date information is to invite an expert to attend the meeting so that he can put members in the picture and answer their questions. Specialists usually attend local government committee meetings to provide up-to-date information and professional advice.

Other useful guidelines when briefing participants are:

1   *Send the information in a brief and condensed form so that it is handy to use.* (The CIA is currently overhauling the way it reports to the White House on international trends. Like executives everywhere, White House officials want sharper, more precise reports to prepare them for important meetings instead of scholarly surveys.)

2   *Check that the information is accurate, and relevant to the problem.* If you have doubts about this, don't send it to the members. If, in the form that the information reaches you, there are a few nuggets buried in a wasteland of irrelevancy, make sure somebody digs them out before they are sent to the members.

3   *Check that the information is reliable* — for instance, that information received from other departments is not merely a camouflage to cover errors or intentions.

4   *Beware of sending information to committee members on a regular basis.* This may cause members to become overloaded with information that becomes less and less relevant as time goes on. The chairman of one committee requested a cost breakdown of a production schedule for a particular meeting. A year later members were still receiving information about production schedules regularly every month.

When briefing members, always aim at giving them a good understanding of the environment in which the problem exists. Reading the working papers should not be an intellectual exercise but a familiarisation exercise: all the information should be pointing straight at the problem, and straight at the alternative solutions.

## Creative and analytical problem-solving

In meetings, as in everyday life, different kinds of problem need to be handled in different ways. For instance, 'creative' and 'analytical' problem-solving require different kinds of leadership and even different kinds of thinkers.* Isn't that the reason why these two types of problem-solving are formally separated in companies? (Manufacturing and R & D, for instance.)

Problems exist that are suited to each of the following methods:

1   *Creative problem solving.* This deals with *(a)* open-ended problems that have no 'correct' answer, e.g. anticipating economic developments or changes in consumer preference, and *(b)* unique or very unusual problems such as a major plant extension, a senior appointment, or how to cope with the effects of the Arab oil embargo.† These problems are unstructured; by their nature, they don't permit the use of any predetermined or structured method. Unique events, because they are without precedent, should be studied from start to finish by very senior men.

The strategy of creative problem-solving is one of trial-and-error, jumping from one approach to another until a *modus operandi* is discovered. This involves a willingness to explore and abandon alternatives very quickly. An idea springs from somebody's lips. It's half-formed, but it takes shape as the others discuss it, ask questions, add to it, turn it upside down. But it still seems inadequate, and is dropped as soon as somebody suggests something else . . . . This is how the method works out in practice.

Obviously, this kind of activity requires minimal structure and a tolerant, supportive atmosphere so that nobody feels inhibited. The chairman controls the proceedings only to the extent necessary to protect members and their ideas from criticism.

2   *Analytical problem-solving.* This deals with problems (often technical or operating problems) which have a 'correct' solution. They are problems of a type frequently encountered in the past, e.g. planning and costing a large building project, and there are known

---

*Research by McKenny and Keen shows that people have different cognitive styles. Some are systematic thinkers, others intuitive thinkers; some receptive thinkers and others perceptive thinkers, etc. They also found that these innate styles greatly affect the way that people do jobs, solve problems, make decisions. See [5.2].

†Very few problems faced by committees are unique or even very unusual. In *The Practice of Management*, Peter Drucker shows that over 90 per cent of decisions made by the management of a large company over a five-year period were 'typical'.

**Table 2**

| | Creative problem-solving | Analytical problem-solving |
|---|---|---|
| 1 Problem type | Deals with problems that have no 'correct' solution and which do not permit the use of a predetermined or structured approach. | Deals with problems that have a 'correct' solution (often technical or operating problems). Thus the aim of the meeting is to structure its proceedings according to a method already known to yield solutions |
| 2 Method | Trial-and-error; exploring and abandoning different alternatives in quick succession; free interaction. | Each element of the problem is systematically analysed; sub-groups may be formed to study different aspects; the recommendations of the sub-groups are integrated into a master plan; cost studies are made and a realistic time schedule drawn up. |
| 3 Control | Minimal structure and control; relaxed atmosphere; no fixed roles. | Careful planning of meeting needed. Structure required to ensure logical sequence; systematic study of the problem and coordination of the various experts. |
| 4 Membership | Members often drawn from different functions and parts of the organisation. This allows a wide range of ideas and expertise to be focused on problem (diversity of thinking helps when problem is unique or very unusual). | Members are often drawn from the same functions or the same group of functions, because specific expertise is often needed to solve technical or operating problems. |
| | ATTRACTS 'DIVERGENT' THINKERS | ATTRACTS 'CONVERGENT' THINKERS |

ways of solving them. *Thus the aim of the meeting should be to structure its activity in terms of a method already known to yield solutions.*

A systematic approach is required. Early in the meeting, members begin by looking for a method, defining constraints, initiating an organised search for information. Then the problem is analysed systematically, stage by stage or aspect by aspect. Often the meeting is split into sub-groups which study particular aspects in detail then report back to the full meeting. Thus there is an increasing refinement of analysis and a gradual movement towards an integrated solution.

Clearly, this kind of activity will only occur if the meeting is carefully planned and structured. The efforts of different experts have to be controlled and coordinated by the man at the centre — the chairman. The style therefore is authoritarian, and this allows expert and relatively quick decisions to be made (although much time may be spent later explaining and winning support for the decisions).

A breakdown of the main differences between creative and analytical problem-solving is shown in Table 2.

## Brainstorming and buzz-groups

As the Strausses have pointed out, brainstorming is based on the theory that 'one man's brainstorm can spark another man's solution' [5.3]. The technique has been used in thousands of companies because it is both highly effective and easy to organise. In many respects it's very like a game for any number of players. More important than numbers is that the participants should be drawn from as wide a range of disciplines and backgrounds as possible so that the ideas produced cover the full spectrum.

The aim is simply to produce as many ideas as possible on a given topic — for instance, how to double the firm's turnover in just twelve months. Every idea is recorded. Absolutely no criticism is allowed. Everybody is encouraged to shoot off any idea that comes into his head, even if it sounds stupid or irrelevant — often an impractical idea becomes practical after a slight modification. The emphasis is on quantity not quality. Analysis and quality-control will follow, after the meeting has ended.

I've always found that provided the atmosphere is relaxed, the participants soon get used to the game and start to enjoy themselves. Enthusiasm and the idea-count soar.

Later, the taped discussion is transcribed into a verbatim report which is carefully scrutinised by a sub-committee for possible leads. The most promising ideas are picked out and, generally, developed by a meeting that is run on more orthodox lines.

Another device for producing quantity rather than quality is the buzz group. You form a buzz group simply by splitting a large meeting into small groups of three or four or five members each, and asking the groups to produce ideas on some topic or to list the main features of the problem as they see it. They then report back to the meeting, say, ten minutes later. This is a good way of quickly testing opinion or of collecting ideas from the entire membership. A lot of ground can be covered; really valuable ideas may emerge; and every member is involved in the problem-solving. Every man immediately finds himself submerged in the problem and contributing to a solution. People who won't open their mouths in a meeting of ten or twelve members, often make a vigorous contribution to small groups.

Another advantage is that buzz groups are easy to organise. There is no need to give instructions about how they should organise themselves or to appoint a chairman for each group, or to tell them where and how you want them to seat themselves. Very small groups always solve these problems for themselves — and very quickly too: for instance, they immediately generate their own leaders.

## A strategy for better solutions

Many a problem-solving meeting turns out to be a kind of tug-o'-war between logic on the one side and emotion and self-interest on the other, with the decision going to the winner of the contest (or emerging from an uneasy compromise). But the outcome can be rendered less fortuitous by this simple strategy, which breaks the meeting into four distinct stages:

1   Study the problem.
2   Generate alternatives.
3   Evaluate the alternatives.
4   Make the decision and forecast the outcome.

When the problem is complex, dealing with each stage in a separate meeting can add to the tidiness of the discussion.

This breakdown follows the 'natural' contours of development in a meeting. Robert Bales and other investigators have discovered that in most meetings there is a natural progression from much information in the first third to much opinion in the middle third and to many suggested solutions in the final third.

The four-stage approach outlined above is a useful aid because the four stages involve quite different kinds of intellectual activity:

1   Analysis (studying the problem).
2   Imagination and creativity (generating alternatives).
3   Criticism (evaluating alternatives).
4   Judgment (making the decision).

All four activities enter into every problem-solving meeting, but usually in a confused and tangled way. The idea of the four-stage strategy is to disentangle the separate activities; to pick out and focus on each one in turn, and in a logical sequence. And so, to use Robert Bales's analogy, the meeting is forced to function like a very efficient communication and control system such as an air-defence network:

> In the military case there are three functions to be performed: *surveillance* of the air by radar, *identification* of the planes as friendly or unknown, and *direction* of fighters sent out to inter-cept unknown planes. These are something like the problems confronting our groups . . . *assembling* the given information on the case, *evaluating* it and *proceeding towards a solution* as the goal. [5.4] *(My italics.)*

The broad principles of structured problem-solving were set down with enduring clarity by John Dewey as long ago as 1910 in *How We Think*. Dewey's deceptively simple questions for problem-solvers were: *(a)* what is the problem, *(b)* what are the alternatives and *(c)* which alternative is best.

## Stage 1: study the problem

The chairman opens the meeting by describing the problem: 'You already know that during our next two or three meetings we shall be considering a proposal for staff rationalisation. In this first meeting could we look at the problem over-all — why it *is* a problem and what the background to it is?' He follows this up by stating the problem as factually as possible and gives costs, turnover statistics and so on, then asks members to add details. (If people are reluctant to speak, why not split the meeting into small buzz groups? Each has five to ten minutes to list the components of the problem as it sees it

*Under time-pressure, decisions are made by high-speed guess*

before reporting back to the meeting.)

This case study approach creates interest and a good understanding of the problem from which, later, a good solution will emerge.

*The trick is to circle round and round the problem before thundering in with a solution;* or before charging off in some particular direction that, towards the end, you realise was the wrong one. And so people who think they know the answer already are tactfully invited to keep their suggestions for Stage 2.

One of the chairman's jobs is to focus attention on key aspects and encourage the meeting to turn them over and over and examine them carefully: 'Could we look at this problem of over-staffing in the typing sections in a bit more detail. As you know, we've been asked to look into the implications of installing a centralised dictation facility, so I've invited Mr Walker of Office Systems to give us some of the facts and figures.' Mr Walker briefs the members, then answers questions.

To round up the discussion in this stage, quickly run over the key factors so that members are left with a clear over-all picture of the problem. Better still, post these key points on a board or wall chart: this will enable the members to keep reminding themselves of the important facts during the rest of the meeting and to see what is missing.

*Stage 2: generate alternatives*

By now the meeting has a good grasp of the problem and ideas for solving it will be bubbling: catch them as they burst and record them for future evaluation. The solution may have to be constructed laboriously, piece by piece, mosaic-like. Or it may emerge in a flash, fully formed.

In the creative process, the irrational component is more important than the rational. Even apparently impractical or even ridiculous suggestions may turn out, after discussion, to contain the seeds of a solution.

*Perhaps success in this stage of the meeting depends on the willingness of the members to take psychological chances and abandon familiar ways of looking at the problem. The meeting may have to discard, or refine, dozens of ideas before it finds one that works.*

Trying again and again is a part of problem-solving. If the search ends too soon the optimum solution may never be born. Yet often we respond to uncertainty by creating false certainty. In a meeting, we quickly select an alternative as the right one — then hunt round feverishly for evidence to justify our choice. But in a problem-solving meeting it is always a mistake to get stuck on one favourite approach. Maier and Hoffman (1960) found that group solutions were of a higher quality when test groups were instructed to find a second solution after they thought they had already solved the problem. Suchman found that it was important to train children from prematurely guessing an explanation of a physical event; for once they had formulated an explanation they had difficulty in revising or dropping it, even when faced with contradictory evidence. How many meetings settle for some inferior solution because they fail to examine enough alternatives?

During this creative stage of the meeting, atmosphere is all-important for it can stimulate creativity or kill it. The climate of the meeting can be stimulating, neutral or destructive, depending largely on the chairman. One way in which he can help to create a supportive atmosphere is by countering critical and destructive comments with such remarks as, 'Before we reject that idea, let's look at its good points first'; and, 'Certainly that idea wouldn't work in this department, but I wonder if it could be made to work in Bill's section'.

The aim is to encourage people to talk freely and cross-fertilise each other's ideas in a tolerant and supportive atmosphere. If this happens, then by a process of free association almost, the ideas begin to spark. Gordon has noted that a 'free-wheeling' group can compress into a few hours the kind of semi-conscious mental activity which might take months of incubation for a single person.

Creative problem-solving involves seeing a problem in a new way. As Hainer and his colleagues have pointed out, a problem is often hard to solve because the participants tend to see new problems as if they were old ones [5.5]:

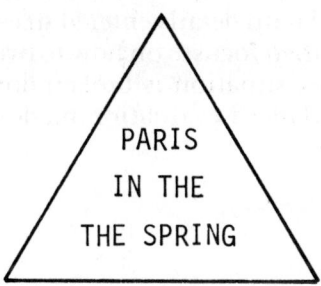

Thus one of the most important chores for the chairman is to stop the meeting from jumping to conclusions by such comments as, 'I quite agree that the production method that you have developed may be exactly right for our purposes. But just before we formally approve it, could we go over the two suggestions made in our last meeting?'

Creative problem-solving involves a willingness to

1  Play with the problem: add to it, subtract from it, turn it over and over and upside down.
2  Forget one aspect and quickly focus on another. Then forget that aspect and look at another. And so on.
3  Deal openly with conflict, hostility, anger in the meeting; and guard against easy compromises (which usually mean low-quality solutions).
4  Tolerate unusual behaviour: 'divergent' thinkers are often mildly deviant. (When I worked in the 'creative' department of an advertising agency, *not* being eccentric in some way or other was a gross deviation.)

Finally, if the meeting gets bogged down, or starts repeating itself, why not take a short break? Sometimes the breakthrough comes immediately after the resumption. Alternatively, adjourn the meeting and give people a chance to sleep on the problem.

*Stage 3: evaluate the alternatives*

Begin this stage of the meeting by reminding members of the alternatives that have emerged. Now, the essential technique is to suspend
judgment while a proper evaluation is made of each alternative.
This can be done by using Norman Maier's two-column method
[5.6]. Two columns are drawn on the blackboard or wall-chart,
headed, respectively, 'Advantages' and 'Disadvantages'. Each alternative is then evaluated with details entered in each of the columns in
turn. The discussion then focuses on how to overcome the disadvantages. Thus a complex situation is broken down into manageable
components and a balanced evaluation made of each one.

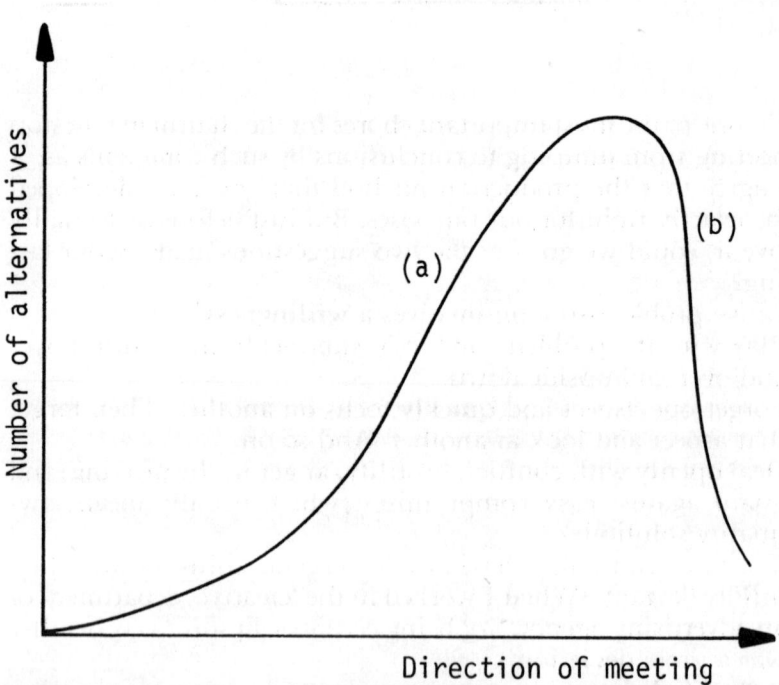

**Figure 8**  *Rational problem-solving in a meeting involves (a) generating
possible solutions then (b) filtering out the less attractive.*

*Stage 4: make the decision*

The alternatives can now be evaluated in order of preference, and the discussion then focuses on how to keep the advantages of the most favoured solution and how to get round the disadvantages; or on whether it would be possible to combine the advantages of two or more of the alternatives.

Once the decision has been made, the ability to forecast the outcomes accurately is very important so that appropriate action can be taken. So the final step is for the meeting to consider questions like these:

1 What *impact* will the decision have, i.e. what parts of the organisation will be affected? How should these departments be informed? How can their cooperation be won?
2 How much will the decision *cost* to implement and what will be the returns? What evidence can we assemble to prove the reliability of our estimates?
3 Whose *help* will we need in implementing the decision?
4 What *resources* will be needed and how do we go about obtaining authorisation for their use?
5 What other *actions* are needed to implement the decision?

**Applying the techniques**

The problem-solving techniques described above are easy to use in actual meetings provided that they are first studied and practised by the chairman, who can then train other members in the methods. (An essential first step is to read Norman Maier's book *Problem-solving Discussions and Conferences* [5.7].) But once mastered, there is no reason why the techniques should not be used at all levels throughout the organisation.

For instance, a group of brickyard foremen learnt the techniques in three one-hour training sessions in Peterborough, and soon after held problem-solving meetings with their own sections. In all cases, the solutions that were reached were accepted by management and successfully implemented. One of these meetings successfully solved a problem that management itself had been trying unsuccessfully to solve for several months. It concerned a scheme for allocating new equipment that was acceptable to the operatives.

The approach to problem-solving outlined here follows the ideas of Norman Maier, Franklyn Haiman, Irving Lee, George Prince and others. Of course, in the open situation of real life, problems frequently do have to be settled in a hurry, on the basis of hunch or rule of thumb, because there simply isn't time for a systematic approach. Thus many major decisions are reached on the basis of inadequate or inconclusive data (Bay of Pigs; the Maplin airport plan). Sometimes, a snap decision can be better than a laboured assessment of all the alternatives. Speed of problem-solving is important in an environment where facts have an unnerving tendency to change their appearance overnight.

But when the problem is big enough and fraught enough, time should be *made* available to ensure that a good solution emerges. Holding problem-solving meetings and running them as they should be run takes up time. But not as much as it takes to unravel all the extra problems that eventually build up as a result of over-hasty decisions.

## Problem-solving techniques

It may be natural for members of a problem-solving committee to solve problems over-casually or on the basis of self-interest — especially in the absence of any clear corporate policy. But it can also damage the organisation. That is why irrational problem-solving needs to be deliberately countered either *(a)* by disciplining those executives who openly use meetings to achieve their own personal ends or *(b)* by instructing committees to discuss the causes and effects of irrational problem-solving and to formulate proposals for overcoming it.

Perhaps problem-solving procedures should be applied more systematically and with greater care in major matters than in minor ones.

New tools such as operational research and statistical analysis can turn problem-solving into a precise science, provided that some of the members of problem-solving committees are equipped with the appropriate quantitative skills. The computer can take the guesswork out of problem-solving, provided that problem-solvers are trained to understand the kind of questions the computer can answer.

*One structural reform that more companies should consider making is to set up an information centre which committee members can ring for information on any aspect of company affairs. Equally good results could come from asking a senior manager to study the*

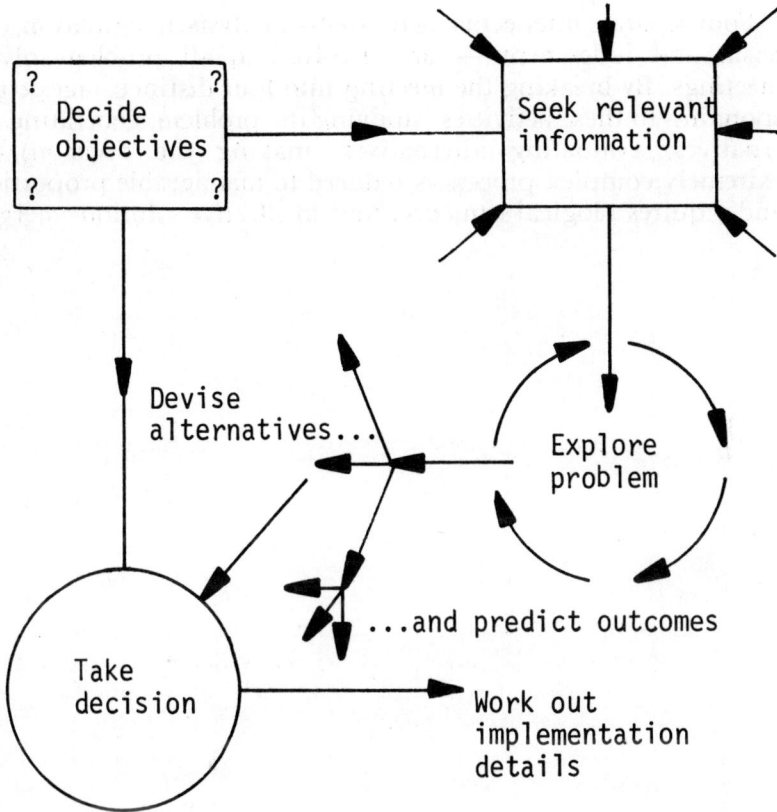

**Figure 9** *Problem solving: the systematic approach.*

*kind of problems dealt with by each company committee so that the information needs of members could be assessed and met by the central administration.*

The use that any particular committee makes of available information depends, of course, on the nature of the problem. For instance, 'creative' problem-solving often requires members to *forget* what they already know, to abandon familiar ways of looking at the problem, and instead to hunt around for a completely new approach, exploring and abandoning alternatives in rapid succession. 'Analytical' problem-solving, on the other hand, deals mainly with technical or operating problems, and a systematic information-search and orderly analysis of the separate components of the problem are usually essential for success.

Four separate intellectual activities — analysis, imagination, criticism and judgement — are involved in all problem-solving meetings. By breaking the meeting into four distinct stages corresponding to these activities (studying the problem; generating alternatives; evaluating alternatives; making the decision), an extremely complex process is reduced to manageable proportions and acquires a logical sequence. And an effective solution emerges.

*An over-elaborate and slow-moving committee system can prolong the decision-making process. Sometimes a new proposal has to pass through two, three or four committees in turn before it is approved. The aim of such idiocy is, as often as not, to protect existing power patterns against the kind of disturbance that innovation and change imply. But in a fast-changing environment, fast decisions are essential for survival.*

# 6
# Streamline your committee system

For many firms in America and Europe, 1974 was shake-out year. The year when problems were surfacing with indecent speed. The year of the stock market collapse, the year of galloping inflation and the energy crisis. Companies that were flexible enough adjusted and survived.

Few companies adjusted as smartly as British Leyland. Senior executives were attending a management seminar when the three-day working week was announced. Suddenly the seminar became a crash course in survival.

A committee was instantly set up. By dawn, it had detailed plans for transport and fuel so that no division would go short, it had established a system of liaison with 2000 suppliers, it had established hot-line links with government agencies. It's nice to know that committees don't *have* to be slow and cumbrous. That they can be as fast and flexible as their members will them to be.

In the United States, Levi Strauss's ready-made clothing firm is another company which relies on fast-moving meetings for survival. Strauss spends a lot of time in meetings discussing changing fashion trends with young employees. 'We get most of our leads on changes in taste and social behaviour patterns from young persons in the company. We're selling most of our output to their contemporaries.'

New product ideas from the top brass have to be vetted by the youngsters before they are rushed to the workshops for translation into cloth. In this company juniors tell seniors what to do — at least some of the time — through the medium of the meeting. And the company benefits from being turned upside down in this way. For these meetings act as a kind of seismograph, allowing the company to sense change almost before it happens.

Meetings are an essential part of this company's survival kit. For in Strauss's world you either adjust quickly to change or you go bust — as a long string of rag-trade bankruptcies in America and Europe in the last decade shows. And not only the clothing industry is vulnerable. Managers in many other industries have to contend with rapidly changing markets and technologies, populations and transportation systems. In many industries, the breakneck pace of technological innovation means that products become obsolete even faster than people unless some device is found to ensure timely replacement.

In modern industry technology is the mighty accelerator that makes change the only constant.* Thus the problems that most managers face have an unnerving tendency to be different tomorrow from what they seemed to be today. That's why you either make committees make their decisions fast or, in the long run, go out of business.

### How to get crowded out of a new market

Imagine that you are a technical manager in a firm that makes electrical household equipment. You've just seen a market research report revealing a shift in consumer preference: a design change in your range of cookers is clearly needed. You work out a plan for new designs with detailed specifications, a time schedule for the development work and a detailed breakdown of costs.

* As Robert Oppenheimer said: 'One thing that is new is the prevalence of newness, the changing scale and the scope of change itself, so that the world alters as we walk on it, so that the years of a man's life measure not some small growth or rearrangement or moderation of what he learned in childhood, but a great upheaval'.

At this stage your proposal is sucked into the committee system. It has to be approved in turn by three screening committees. You find a champion on Committee A who pushes the proposal through without much delay. (The minute reads: *'Resolved:* that the proposal as set out in document X be submitted to Committee B for their consideration'.)

Committee B haggles over minor details and sends the proposal back to your office for revision. You do this and resubmit the plan. Weeks later Committee B takes another look and this time approves it. (The decision is duly minuted: *'Resolved:* that the revised proposal as set out in document X should be submitted to the Projects Committee for approval'.)

Your final hurdle — the Projects Committee. It alone can authorise development work and vote funds. But this august body is manned by six very senior, very conservative managers who gladly support all new proposals as long as they combine low investment risk with guaranteed commercial success, i.e. none of them! (They frown on all others.) They know the cash value of everything and the true value of nothing (so instinctively clip the wings of high flyers). In their first meeting the gentlemen can't agree. In the second they concede that the proposal has some merits (especially low development costs) and grudgingly nod consent.

But by this time six months have limped by. Conditions have changed. Indeed, a thick chunk of your potential market has already been sliced off by a smaller and zippier rival who saw his chance late but acted on it instantly.

This story is, I suspect, fairly typical. It gives a clue as to why so many important technical and marketing breakthroughs are made by the smaller companies. The Wankel engine, for instance, was developed by a small German organisation and perfected by a small Japanese car maker who knew the commercial value of fast decision-making. (While this was going on the giant American car makers were busy not listening to those maverick managers who were shouting in meetings about a big domestic upsurge in demand for small cars.)

*The moral is clear. Any large company working in a fast-changing environment needs a simple committee system. One that can take decisions and authorise changes as soon as the need for them becomes clear. Consider the example of the British engineering company which split its elaborate committee system into several smaller systems, each one making decisions independently about a clearly defined range of problems. Admittedly, there was some loss of coor-*

*dination between different functions. But decision-making became fast and flexible.* Now, only *one* committee needs to vet a new proposal before work gets done on it. As a result the company reports that it finds it easier and quicker to adjust to change than at any time in the past.

### Adjust — or bust

Management must learn to cope with change or expect a change of management. Their decision-making machinery needs to be lubricated with greased lightning. Once a new problem or opportunity is seen, the manager should be able to rush to the nearest decision point for *quick* action.

But in many large firms, the decision-making machinery works very slowly. John Hacket has pointed to the 'increasing number of cases in which the managements of large well-regarded companies face financial emergencies because their control systems detected serious problems only after they had reached crisis proportions' — and presumably these 'systems' include finance, progress and other kinds of committee [6.1].

Sometimes, the hierarchical nature of the decision-making pro-

*Some committees have to be made to make faster decisions*

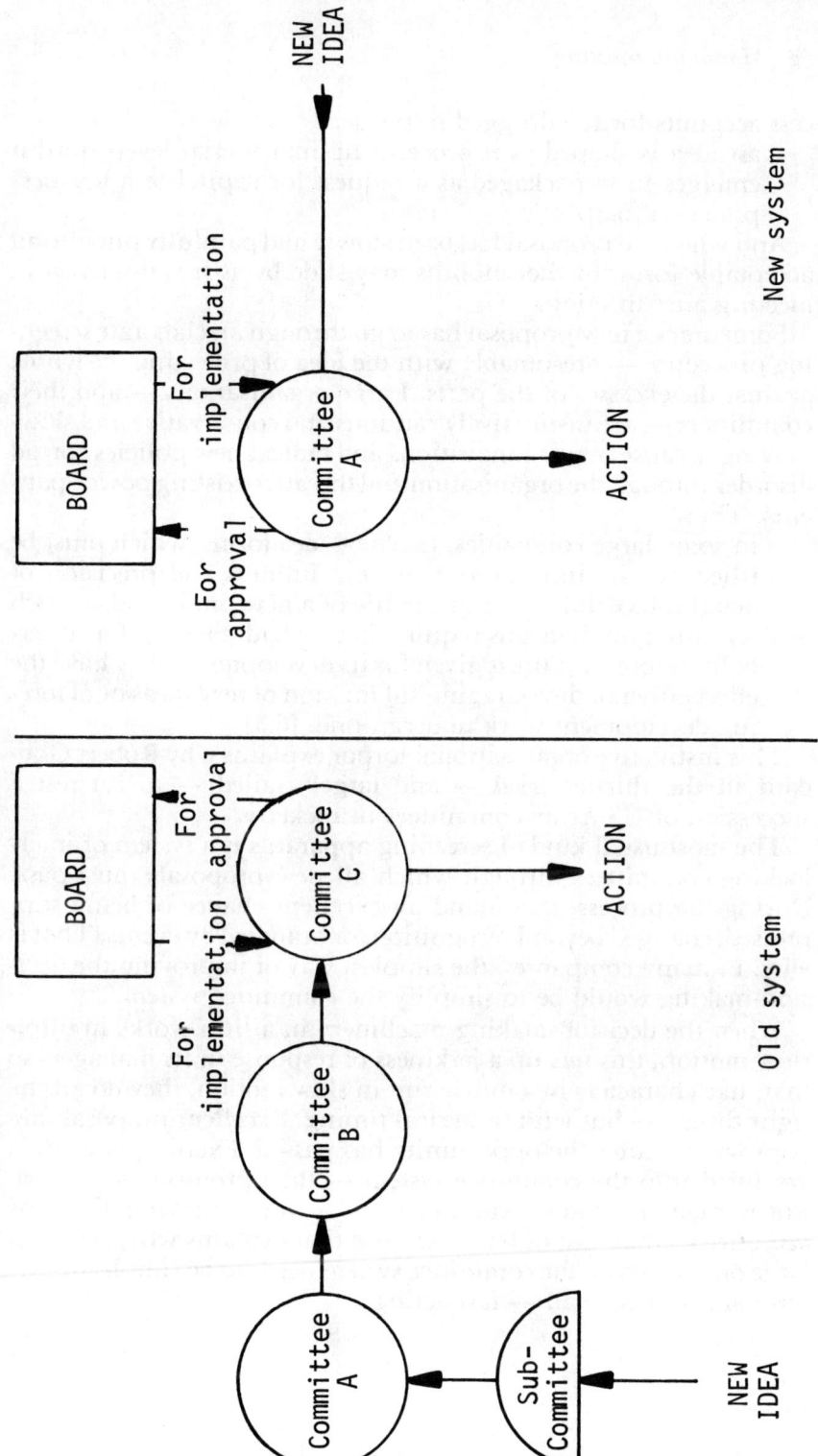

**Figure 10** *By simplifying its committee system, one company cut the time taken to approve and implement new proposals by several months. Each committee was given decision-making powers within a carefully defined area instead of having to pass on recommendations to some higher body.*

cess accounts for the drugged response:

> an idea is shaped as it proceeds up managerial levels until it emerges fully packaged as a request for capital or a business plan . . . : [6.2]

And when the proposal has been slowly and painfully put into an acceptable form, further months may slide by as it is discussed in meeting after meeting.

Sometimes a new proposal has to go through an elaborate screening procedure — presumably with the idea of protecting the whole against the excesses of the parts. Large organisations — and their committees — are instinctively cautious and conservative and slow-moving because major innovations and radical new policies spread disorder through the organisation and threaten existing power-patterns. Thus:

> in some large companies, the 'new idea forms' which must be filled out by innovators require a fullness and precision of detail impossible early in the life of a new product idea. Such screening mechanisms require that each idea be developed verbally before support is given for its development; they have the effect either of discouraging submission of new ideas or of forcing development work underground. [6.3]

This instinctive organisational torpor explains why Robert Goddard in the thirties tried — and largely failed — to interest a succession of US Army committees in rocketry.

The most usual kind of screening apparatus is a system of interlocking committees through which all new proposals must pass. During the process, they stand an excellent chance of being suppressed, changed beyond recognition, or outdated by events. That is why, in many companies, the simplest way of improving the decision-making would be to simplify the committee system.

When the decision-making machinery in a firm works in ultra-slow motion, this sets up a jerkiness of response in its managers so that, like characters in a movie run in slow motion, they do all the right things — but with hysterical timing. Excellent proposals are approved — after the opportunity has passed. Exciting new ideas are lured into the committee system — then promptly strangled. But in modern business you must find a way of making decisions *fast* or risk going out of business. And that explains why, even in a large organisation, the committee system needs to be simple, innovative and — above all — fast-acting.

*Follow the guidelines below to sharpen the impact that you make on meetings. This chapter explains how to improve your status in the committee; how to win support for your proposals; how to beat the opposition by anticipating their attacks; and how to kill a proposal with the gentle touch.*

# 7
# Participating

Join me at a meeting called to discuss the fuel crisis caused by the Arab oil embargo. An English engineering company. A day in January 1974. Room temperature: a patriotic 55°F.

Speaker after speaker bewails the awesome dimensions of the problem, tells frightening tales of mass bankruptcies and the looming world recession. Only one element is missing: constructive suggestions.

Then a young manager begins to talk. He has done his homework thoroughly, and the others sit up as he spells out a plan for allocating the reduced fuel supplies between departments so that there will be no crimps in production, even with the squeeze hard on. These ideas stimulate other suggestions, and members begin to develop the proposal.

A week later, the plan goes into action.

*Careful preparation allows even the young and inexperienced to make an impact on a meeting and to influence the decision-makers.*

*It ensures that quality of presentation matches the quality of the idea.* When none of the members is properly prepared or adequately briefed, decisions get made by High Speed Guess. This frequently happens on local government committees — and incidentally raises the question whether laymen are the right people to take decisions on such complex matters as education and town planning.

Prepare for meetings by carefully reading all pre-circulated working papers. Study the agenda. Which items are the important ones? Thoroughly brief yourself on these topics so that you don't waste the meeting's time by needlessly asking for information or by talking off the top of your head.

Prepare notes for use as a speaking aid. Make certain that your facts are accurate because a single detected error will weaken your case. (Two or three can destroy it.) Use plenty of examples and illus-

```
ITEM 7: FUEL POLICY


1  Oil costs rising exponentially
   (a) Continuing trend
       - supply and demand
   (b) Next 5 years
       - CBI
       - Economic Intelligence Unit
       - Department of Trade figures


2  Gas, electricity, coal - steadier rise
   (a) Gas: installation costs
       - favourable credit terms
   (b) Electricity: installation
       - about half existing equipment still
         serviceable
```

**Figure 11**  *Suggested notes format*

trations and case histories. People are more interested in people —
and specific cases — than in abstract argument. If time allows and
the issue is important enough, write out all the points you plan to
make in full. Then condense this script to brief notes and practice
speaking from them. I have always found notes arranged in a series
of headings and sub-headings, as shown in Figure 11, especially
easy to follow.

Some people find reminder cards less distracting than notes, each
card containing a heading and two or three supporting points.

The value of notes is that a quick glance at a word or phrase will
remind you of a whole string of associated ideas because of the preparation that has gone into them. Thus you can expand each brief
note to almost any length you like.

Prepare any charts, handouts or other visual aids well in advance.
These add impact and make what you say more interesting. During
the meeting, keep these aids out of sight until you are ready to use
them, and clear them away as soon as you have finished with them.
But *over*-preparation has its dangers. It can make you misjudge a
complex issue so that you arrive at the meeting thinking you know
all the answers. There's a lot of difference between coming to a meeting armed with information and coming armed with conclusions.
(People accept information, but reject conclusions.) And too great
an input of information can create an overload effect. In one experiment, members of discussion groups were given either two, four or
six possible solutions to a human relations problem. Usually the
member with only two alternatives dominated his group both in
quantity and quality of contributions.

### The manager's guide to lobbying

The most important kind of preparation for a meeting is squaring
other people — assessing support for your proposals, testing opinion, lobbying, convincing the other participants. Discuss your proposals before the meeting with as many of the other members as
possible. Assess their reactions: people will either state their opinions openly or ask you questions which are clues to their attitudes.
Thus you learn if your proposal has any chance of acceptance;
whether you should present it to the meeting or quietly drop it.

Leave the bigot off your calling list when lobbying. No matter
what you say to him, he'll continue to see your proposal through
the focus of his own prejudices, refuse to accept compromise, go

along to the meeting with a closed mind. But by integrating other people's ideas into your proposal you may be able to strengthen it and to increase its chance of acceptance. And other people's comments will reveal weak points and gaps in your thinking that you would otherwise have missed.

Lobbying soon teaches you that people don't always see things the way they are. Into every situation they read their own romance. They 'perceive information or reinterpret data in the direction of their motivation and wishes. People hear what they want to hear, forget what they want to forget' [7.1]. So that even if your case is strong and watertight, other people may not recognise the fact. They have to be convinced. Or, rather, they have to convince themselves. For, as Lewin has shown, groups change their minds by a three-stage process: *(a)* unfreezing of previous attitude, *(b)* change in attitude, *(c)* freezing of new attitude. This means that if members are to accept your proposal they must first become aware of the weakness of their present way of thinking. This won't happen if you are too forceful and uncompromising, for members won't 'hear' you correctly: you will be psychologically distant: your ideas will be too alien to fit into their present pattern of thinking. That is why, from the lobbying stage onward, you need to gently encourage members to draw conclusions about weaknesses in their present thinking — and invite them to use your ideas to fill in the holes. Show a spirit of compromise by being willing to meet their objections by adjusting your proposal; or, even better, by being willing to integrate their suggestions into your proposal.

## Six-point plan

Prepare your case thoroughly and systematically by following this six-point plan:

*1 Thoroughly research the subject.* Familiarise yourself with the background to the problem. Collect all the information that you and the other participants will need to make a decision. Be sure to be completely accurate with your facts: a single inaccuracy can destroy faith in your proposal.

*2 Inform the committee secretary* (or otherwise the meeting organiser) of your intention to present an important proposal at the next meeting, so that he has time to arrange for working papers to be drawn up and circulated, and so that the item can be included on the agenda.

*3 Prepare the opposition case* by anticipating likely objections. Then prepare counter-arguments.

*4 Lobby the other participants.* If you haven't time to see them all, see the most influential (usually the most senior men: nothing helps you more than having allies in high places). Explain your proposal to them. If necessary, adjust your position to ensure greater support. If your proposal is obviously unacceptable, quietly drop it.

*5 Circulate a memo* to all members stating your revised proposal in detail. Provide full supporting evidence.

*6 During the meeting, hammer home the main points and the main benefits of your proposal* — members have already read the details in your memo. Even at this late stage be willing to incorporate other people's suggestions into the proposal — they may strengthen it and make it more acceptable.

Careful preparation and presentation greatly increase the chance that your proposal will be accepted. Often the facts refuse to speak for themselves in a meeting, and only skilful communication can ram home their significance.

Acceptability is just one of the reasons for being flexible in meetings and looking for areas of agreement. For you can never have it all your own way. Rather, you need to learn from others and incorporate their ideas into your proposals so that a superior — or at least, workable — solution emerges. Engels pointed out that in history 'the final result always arises from conflict between many individual wills.... What each individual wills is obstructed by everyone else, and what emerges is something that no one wanted.' Hence the pained consensus smile of the practised committeeman. Perhaps subordinating your own ends to the objectives of the group (or of people you represent) is, in any case, a higher level of participation. Self-centred individuals who strive to win purely personal victories in meetings can be very disruptive, and may subvert organisational goals.

(For a quick indication of whether individuals in a meeting are group-centred or self-centred, count how many times they say 'we'

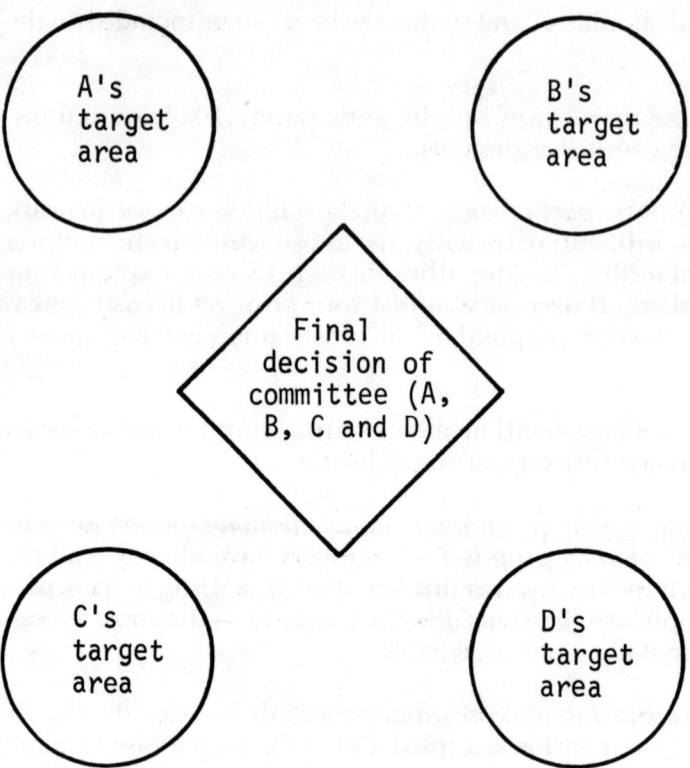

**Figure 12** *'What each individual wills is obstructed by every body else, and what emerges is something that no one wanted.' Be prepared to incorporate other people's ideas into your proposals — or to see them defeated.*

as opposed to 'I'. Researchers have found that the frequent use of 'we' in meetings leads to feelings of satisfaction among the members.)

**Counter-attacking**

Anybody who proposes major changes in the organisation becomes a universal target for attack and criticism. People resist change and oppose important proposals made in meetings almost by instinct. Often the virulence of these attacks makes the proposer himself lose faith in the proposal. But the trouble with this ferocious conservatism is that good and potentially workable ideas are blocked, opportunities for new methods and breakthroughs lost to the company.

The best tactic for beating off opposition attacks is to anticipate them: try to predict the various objections then prepare an answer to them. For instance, almost every major proposal meets with the objections that *(a)* it won't work or *(b)* it's too expensive. But once you know that this sort of attack is likely to be made on your proposal it becomes a fairly simple matter to work out a decisive counter-attack:

*First attack*: We can't afford it.

*Counter-attack*: I've examined the financial aspect because I was rather concerned about it too. But it turns out that *we* can afford it. Here are the figures.

*Or*: We can't afford *not* to do it. Think of all the benefits. (*Go on and list them.*)

*Second attack:* It isn't in the budget.

*Counter-attack:* It *should* be in the budget. On the other hand, it's a completely new idea so I suppose you wouldn't expect it to be. If the proposal is implemented it will lead to substantial savings in the following areas .... These will more than cover the cost of implementation.

*Third attack:* It's been tried before — and it was a failure. It just won't work.

*Counter-attack:* Last time the circumstances were completely different and the plan itself was different. (*List the differences.*)

*Or:* Last time it was introduced prematurely and badly implemented.

*Or:* I'm surprised that you think it won't work because I've discussed the plan with Shaw, Jones and Wells who will have to carry it out if we approve it. They all feel that it's perfectly feasible. But if you can suggest any ways of making it *easier* to implement ....

If, despite these counter-attacks, it seems that your proposal will be rejected, fall back on your last line of defence: find a reason for *delaying* the decision. Ask for a postponement so that you can assemble more information, consult somebody, find the answer to certain questions. The extra time will give you time to strengthen your case and do some intensive lobbying.

If you care less about getting a particular proposal accepted than about winning a political or symbolic victory over the enemy, why not suddenly change your position once it is clear that your proposal will be rejected: 'You seem to have got the impression that I'm proposing a merger of the two sections. On the contrary, I think it is important to keep each section independent'. This blasts the ground from under the enemy's feet and leaves them either foolishly agreeing with you after all, or — even more foolishly — persisting in their opposition in spite of your turnaround.

## Study your colleagues

The need to anticipate people's reactions to your proposals and their possible lines of attack explains why you should get to know the personal and group characteristics of your committee colleagues as soon as possible. Once you know the sort of people they are you will be able to take the approaches which, with that particular group, get the best results. Find out what you can about them. Study them during meetings — their strong and weak points, the way they react to different ideas. If this sounds hard and unfeeling remember that they are scrutinising you with equal intensity.

What is each man's position in the status league? Who are the unofficial leaders? What are the various specialisms and functions of the members? Is anybody likely to take a particular line on any particular issue? Is the committee as a whole cautious or radical in approach? What kind of proposals will it and won't it accept? Collect all this information systematically and deliberately so that you don't ride into battle unarmed.

Find out which members are, secretly or openly, committed to representing special interests, e.g. a trade union or a particular department, or a clique of managers. This knowledge will tell you which people and which topics need to be approached with special care.

Learn as much about your committee colleagues as possible so that you will neither overestimate nor underestimate them — both dangerous mistakes. Knowing their strengths and weaknesses you will be able to adopt the most effective tactics for dealing with them.

## Roles

You have been asked to sit on a company committee and you want to make a useful contribution — but how? Begin by asking yourself these questions:

1    Am I expected to play the same role as my predecessor, e.g. the

ideas man, or the sound, no-nonsense executive? Do I wish to play this role? If so, how can I play it effectively?

2 Have I been invited to join the committee because of my competence in a particular area? If so, I am expected to play a specialist role, contributing expertly and decisively in certain areas, therefore I must be extremely well briefed in these areas.

3 Am I expected to play a representative role by always speaking on behalf of a department or some special interest or a group of people? If so, how can I keep in touch with the opinions of the people I represent? And how can I keep them informed about what the committee is thinking and doing? (These questions are particularly difficult to answer when the represented group is a large one.)

Be clear about the kind of role you are expected to play. Is this the kind of role you are able and willing to play? On several occasions I have discovered that the new boy on the committee is pushed into a particular role by the needs and expectations of the moment, and determined resistance is needed if the role is one that you don't want to play.

*Roles are established early in the life of a committee.** The members need roles to help them communicate with each other and to make mutual relationships less shifting and uncertain.* Without roles, they would never be sure that they were speaking to someone with the correct degree of familiarity, or that they weren't speaking out of turn or trespassing in somebody else's area of responsibility. Role-playing forces the members to gear their individual behaviour to that of their committee colleagues. This gives the committee a systematic quality and provides a convenient mechanism for ensuring stability and certainty in the group.

Brian Mitchell has suggested that people in meetings need roles in order to create the illusion that the father-chairman loves each of them for a particular quality that they display. He further argues that a few basic roles, which are played in all groups, together express the full range of human instincts [7.3]. For instance, there are always several people who have to be out of favour in a committee because the group needs a target for its instinctive aggressions.

But what are the basic roles? Mitchell draws an analogy with a medieval court:

*King.* The authority figure who takes the final decisions.

---

* P.E. Slater notes that rather stable role differentiations sometimes emerge within the first few hours of a group's existence [7.2].

*Queen.* Has limited areas of authority. Occasionally checks the King's autocratic powers.

*Jester and Buffoon.* Their clowning is an unconscious attempt to relieve the tensions and hostilities of the group.

*Prophet.* He gets satisfaction from the prestige of being the group's critic. If his prophecies prove wrong he may become the

*Scapegoat,* who carries the sins of the group on his shoulders. A scapegoat is needed because members need to be able to attribute all intra-group tensions to one person so that, by expelling him, they symbolically expel all their troubles too. Often the expulsion fails to relieve group tensions so that, immediately, a new scapegoat is needed.

## Experiment with roles

Committee members realign their roles continually as their own needs and those of the group change. In a dynamic, developing committee, a member will try most of the available roles, one after the other. Perhaps, optimum performance of the committee depends on all the members finding roles which really suit them. Certainly, when roles stabilise in the committee there is usually a dramatic increase in cohesiveness and efficiency — perhaps because people can then concentrate all their energies on the task.

Boost the quality of your committee work by deliberately experimenting with roles — the expert, the genial socialiser, the man of action, the coordinator, the conciliator, and so on — until you find one that suits you most of all.* A very important role is played by any individual who links the committee to key parts of the organisation. In the Forecasting Committee, for instance, the systems manager is likely to be king.

## Pecking order

Every committee develops a definite pecking order in terms of the amount of speech and influence permitted. For instance, if you have little status you can't interrupt higher-status members when they are speaking but they are free to interrupt you. Only high-status per-

* 'A member does not take a role in the sense that we might say he took leadership, but rather he tries out for a role and is awarded or denied it by the others', say Howell and Bormann [7.4].

*The scapegoat on the committee carries the sins of the group on his shoulders*

sons are allowed to express key opinions — for instance, that there should be a change of membership. *Proposals from low-ranking people are brushed aside unless they find a high-ranking champion to defend them. Low-status members typically confine their contributions to requests for information and opinions and to expressions of agreement and disagreement.*

Your place in the hierarchy depends largely on how useful you have been to the committee in the past. That is why the new boy finds himself at the bottom of the ladder — he has no past. So little notice is taken of what he says. By a subtle system of rewards and punishments the group keeps him in his place, makes him keep a civil tongue, even — in the long run — makes him think and speak like itself. This process is accelerated when the newcomer *pretends* to share the group's values from the start. Cognitive dissonance theory suggests that if a person says or does something which contradicts his attitude, he tends to modify his attitude so that the inconsistency is eliminated. Eventually you become what you pretend to be.

During a meeting the deviant member has a great deal of communication directed at him in an attempt to make him get into line: but if he persists in his nonconformity the group may reject him at the end.

*Group pressure keeps the new boy in his place*

There is a gradual convergence towards shared ways of perceiving and judging. Hence the common experience of representatives on a committee (including the House of Commons) being absorbed by the committee and drifting away from the people they represent. As Michael Argyle points out, the newcomer moves from *compliance* to *internalisation* of group norms. Lewin showed that even those individuals who are highly resistant to influence by other individuals are usually susceptible to group persuasion. And chronic nonconformists — people who resist even the group — tend to crack up in the end.

### Climbing the ladder

The penalty of belonging is loss of independence. That is why the newcomer to the committee has a vitally important role to play — that of the 'new thinker' and the independent critic. Psychologically an outsider, the newcomer may be the only man on the committee who can actually see the flaws and shortcomings in a particular proposal, the only man who can see a way of twisting out of a crisis or of cutting costs or finding new business.

But nobody listens. He may have clear vision and new ideas, but nobody wants to know because he's nobody. To win acceptance for his ideas and proposals he needs status fast — before he is absorbed by the committee and becomes like all the rest, i.e. blinkered. The only way to beat the system is to appear to join it. Incidentally, for a quick impression of who already has high status, note who is looking at whom: those who receive the most looks are usually the most powerful.

Who looks at whom seems to relate to power coalitions. Those who look most at a speaker are rated by him as instrumental to his goals. Those looked at most by the speakers are seen by others and themselves as being more powerful in the group than those who are looked at less. See Weisbrod [7.5].

Body relaxation is also another important indicator of status: the more relaxed participants are likely to be those with the highest status in the committee. Thus body signals pierce the camouflage of procedure and convention and unconsciously reveal psychological truths.

Through the decades, loyal selfless service alone will give you influence. But by that time your critical faculty has been blunted and your ideas have changed — become institutionalised: reasons enough for wishing to speed your upward climb.

In the crucial early stages of your membership, members are judging whether or not you are worth listening to from your appearance and manner. Whether or not you are acceptable in the early stages may depend on the clothes you wear, the way your hair is cut, your party manners. By such trivia as these men win each other's confidence and respect. (Good grooming is particularly important in older men.)

The amount of preparation you do will largely determine whether the seasoned members will ignore you or listen with respect. And in early meetings, simply talking can establish you in the status hierarchy by winning you a reputation for productivity. The Laboratory of Social Relations at Harvard has been studying meetings and small groups for nearly 30 years. Surprisingly, it concludes that talkative members usually contribute the most helpful remarks and have the best ideas and that other members recognise this.

If your committee colleagues judge you productive in early meetings they will expect you to be productive in later meetings too. This expectation increases your confidence at the time when you need it most. Moreover, success in winning acceptance for an idea stimulates you to put more ideas forward and to think of ways of making them acceptable: so gradually you establish yourself as a dynamic and capable member of the committee.

The price to be paid is that if you continue being productive and talkative in meeting after meeting, you lose friends and influence people. You may become influential but you lose popularity. Productivity is resented — perhaps because it is felt as a kind of control.

Participate early and make your presence felt throughout the meeting. Deliberately break away from personal preoccupations as soon as the meeting starts. Focus hard on the topic for discussion. Assemble your thoughts, and contribute. The earlier you do this, the greater your total contribution is likely to be, and this will boost your reputation for productivity. But sometimes it is better to reserve your contribution until later in the discussion. For instance, you may wish to state your case immediately before the vote so that there can be no hard-hitting replies.

## The right tactics

Speed your climb up the status hierarchy by
1    Careful preparation for meetings, i.e. self-briefing, case-preparation, lobbying.
2    Establishing a reputation for productivity by early and frequent contributions.
3    Demonstrating independent judgement and innovative thinking, both of which should come easily to a new member.
4    Ensuring that your personal appearance and manner inspire respect during the first meetings that you attend.
5    Listening to others in meetings and being willing to incorporate their ideas into your proposals.
6    Carrying out any assignments which stem from meetings with thoroughness and vigour.

Another reason for adopting these approaches is that every time you participate in a meeting you are demonstrating your ability to think and analyse. Thus by taking the trouble to develop your committee skills you automatically develop your managerial ability at the same time. The ability to contribute effectively in meetings not only helps you to get your ideas accepted and to pass on your specialist knowledge, but also demonstrates your capacity for higher responsibility. Even if things go wrong and you fail to impress, there is the consolation of knowing that failure can be more valuable than success. As Antony Jay has pointed out, success only makes you preen yourself, but failure makes you think about *why* you failed — where you went wrong and the principles you violated.

## The gentle art of opposition

When Wesley lashed his audiences they wept and trembled and were converted. The history of parliamentary and congressional debates shows that invective and diatribe are effective ways of killing a proposal. But direct attack is only effective when the assault party is strong enough to fight off the counter-attack that is inevitably provoked. For when people feel that they are being criticised or attacked, they stop listening and instead prepare an elaborate self-justification, or plan a withering counterblast; cooperative problem-solving stops. That is why the most effective form of opposition in a meeting is not to criticise your opponent but to show him pleasantly and tactfully how his proposal could be strengthened.

Use the ABC approach to make criticism acceptable — Agree, Befriend, Compliment —

*Agree with some of the details of the proposal before rejecting the main theme:* 'I think the idea of charging the commercial rate for our PR booklets is an extremely interesting one; and we should certainly look carefully at the proposal to set up a special PR section. But I don't think that we can solve this problem simply by improving the PR operation.'

*Befriend the proposer by using friendly queries to express your doubts, instead of making him an enemy by direct criticism:* 'Jack, you say the system would only cost £2000, but wouldn't there be extra costs because of training? . . . Do you think this would require extra space, because we're already overcrowded? . . . Would this mean renting more accommodation?' The proposer will see your friendly query not as an attack but as a request for further information. Trying to supply this information may make him have second thoughts about his own proposal.

*Compliment the proposer on his objectives. Then, in a friendly way, say that you doubt whether his proposal will achieve them:* 'I think your idea of involving our employees in the decision-making and giving them more control over working conditions is a very good one — it's something we should have been talking about years ago. But I don't think that the sort of committee you've described would have this effect.'

The ABC approach enables you to criticise your committee colleagues without antagonising them; to attack their proposals, but
without provoking a counter-attack.

The critic needs the gentle touch because the chief characteristic
of criticism is its negativeness. Usually the criticised person feels
put down and his sense of worth and satisfaction are injured. He
reacts defensively with self-justification, or aggressively with counter-attack, which puts an end to cooperative problem-solving. Too
much time in meetings is taken up in fault-finding and hole-pick-
ing. Often, the hurt feelings that are caused —

> are translated unconsciously into uncooperative or even aggres-
> sive behaviour aimed at the person who has stepped on one's
> toes. In a meeting such action is usually disguised as a rational
> and potentially useful contribution to the dialogue. [7.6]

### Restate, and ask for examples

Hesitate, in any case, before disagreeing with what somebody says.
Often it is a good idea to restate the point you object to in your own
words, to make sure that you have understood:

> *You:* I think what you're saying is that the new system would
> pay for itself in the first twelve months because of the extra
> productivity . . . .
> *Proposer:* Not exactly that: I said that some firms have found
> that it pays for itself within twelve months — not only because
> of the extra productivity, but also because of the reduction in
> staff that is possible.

The area of disagreement either disappears, or becomes more shar-
ply defined so that the discussion gains in point and precision.

Similarly, don't use or disagree with the big statement, the grand
generalisation of the 'employers are only interested in one thing —
profits' type. Otherwise conflict will be generated out of mere
words. Wait for the specific instances, the concrete examples,
because they contain the substance of what the other member is saying: 'Employers are only interested in one thing —
profits . . . . You've only got to to look at the way management
treated our last pay claim.' You waited for the specific example, and
the argument turned out to be a very specific and factual one about a
recent pay claim, not something wide and abstract. If specific examples are not forthcoming, ask for them.

## Full frontal assault

If your gentler efforts fail but you remain convinced that the proposal is wrong and must be stopped at all costs, you may have to risk full frontal assault — the aim of which is to make your opponent fold his tenets and steal into the night. But do this only if you have enough support or status in the meeting to survive the inevitable counter-attack. The following direct methods of attack are especially effective when supported by detailed evidence:

*1   Attack the* morality *of the proposal.* The proposers are misguided in their thinking and wrong in their aims. The proposal must be rejected at all costs. If approved, it would deprive employees of any control over their working conditions. No committee, in the 1970s, has the right to do that.

*2   Attack the* cost *aspect.* The costs, as stated, are alarming. If anything, they have been underestimated. For instance, surely the following items need to be taken into account.... It may be a desirable scheme, but it would be ruinously expensive to carry out. Could the proposers enlighten the committee and explain where the money is to come from, because it has not been included on any budget? The committee has no authority to approve it.

*3   Express doubts about the* practicality *of the proposal.* The proposal can't possible work. The necessary equipment and the necessary expertise just aren't available. Moreover, it isn't a new idea: it's been tried before, and it proved a complete flop. The proposal must be rejected because the risk of failure is so great.

*4   Question the* reliability *of available information.* The information we've been given is incomplete. For instance, nobody really knows how the employees feel about the proposal. Moreover, there are inaccuracies and half-truths in the evidence before us: the proposers have admitted that the time-schedule they propose is rather uncertain, and that their costing is optimistic. Indeed, it seems to me that the costs could easily be much higher. We can't possibly approve the scheme until we have far more precise and reliable evidence to go on.

*5   Attack the* proposers *and point out what they stand to gain by the proposal.* Hint at interest and partiality; at empire-building and behind-stage wheeling. Try to show that their gain is other people's loss — in particular, other people on the committee.

*6 Make him specify before he's ready to.* Ask for specific details and explanations when he's deliberately being general and dealing in outlines. If he tries to give you the details he'll probably get so involved and muddled that the other members will lose faith in his proposal.

## The meaning of teamwork

Careful preparation is the key to effective participation in meetings. This may involve:

1 Briefing yourself on key topics.
2 Informing the committee secretary of your intention to present an important proposal at the next meeting.
3 Lobbying the other participants to explain your proposal and to assess support (lobbying also enables you to anticipate any opposition attacks so that you have time to prepare a decisive answer).
4 Sending a memo to all members with your proposal spelled out in detail.

Boost the quality of your participation by deliberately experimenting with roles — coordinator, socialiser, man of action, ideas man, expert, chairman's right-hand man, conciliator, and so on — before deciding which one suits you most. Every newcomer to a committee, though, is potentially capable of playing the vital role of Independent Critic because, psychologically, he is still an outsider.

Participating early and frequently in meetings wins you a reputation for productivity. You can boost this reputation by ensuring that any assignments stemming from meetings are carried out with thoroughness and vigour.

Being willing to incorporate other people's ideas into your proposals, and using the ABC approach to make your criticisms acceptable, permit forceful and effective participation without creating antagonism in the other members. Effective participation in meetings means being emotionally and intellectually involved in the subject and sensitive to the feelings of the other members.

Like it or not, in most modern organisations you have to participate in meetings in order to achieve your goals. Participation gives you the chance to make your talents and experience available to the entire organisation: it is your chance to influence the decision-makers and to demonstrate your high-flying executive qualities. That is why committeemen who have the desire — and the ability — to present their own ideas to advantage, and to criticise other people's without offending them, are well placed to increase their status and influence in the organisation.

*Meetings are an expensive activity. But generally the high running costs are tolerated because nobody is instructed to find out just how high they are. An effective way of cutting running costs is to ask each committee to calculate them then to slash this figure in half. Or ask a senior manager to do a sharp-pencil operation on all company committees to see where savings could be made. Startling savings can be made simply by shortening the length of meetings (like the company which limited all meetings to 20 minutes), and by holding them only when there is a specific problem to be solved.*

# 8
# How to cut running costs

In most companies the problem is not to eliminate meetings but to manage them more efficiently — and efficiency means boosting productivity and cutting running costs. Don't let this be said about any of the meetings that you organise: 'Never has so little been said in so many words by so many so often'.

Startling savings can be made by shortening the length of meetings. Bowater felt so sure of this that at one time it limited all meetings to 20 minutes. Air-France compresses meetings into two short daily slots: 9-11 and 11-1. The President of an American bank has developed his own highly personal brand of time control. He has an iron rule, and keeps to it: after precisely two hours in a meeting he gets up in mid-sentence, says 'Good day' to the assembled company and retires. The meeting has ended.

An extremely useful gadget for making people in meetings more cost-conscious is an electronic clock that adds up the pay-rate of those attending and gives a second-by-second account of the cost to the company. Even such a simple device as this can stimulate snappier, more productive meetings. Equally effective was the tape recorder smuggled into a meeting by the chairman of Dow Chemicals. Later he played the tape back to the participants. All agreed that if they had stuck to essentials and if there had been no waffling or diversions, the meeting could have been cut to a few minutes. This would have represented a saving to the company of several thousand dollars.

## The cost-benefit problem

A recurring problem in many organisations is that too many people spend *too much* time in meetings. Perhaps the biggest single reason why this happens is that nobody is ever given the job of costing the operation and weighing this figure against the benefits. Almost every other aspect of a company's activities is subjected to stringent cost-benefit analysis, but not meetings. And the result is thousands of inefficient — and expensive — meetings.

Consultant James Rice, for instance, has studied meetings in a hundred large firms and he reckons that no more than one in ten works efficiently. According to Rice, many meetings should never be called at all, and many items placed before committees could be better dealt with by normal administrative means. When Rosemary Stewart surveyed 160 British managers it turned out that they spent about half their time in formal or informal discussions.* Yet according to an American consultant, Alec Mackenzie, nine out of ten businessmen reckon that half the time spent in meetings is wasted.

Meetings are an expensive activity. After all, each senior man who attends a meeting in a large American company, say, may be costing the company up to two dollars a minute. Admittedly, group decisions are often superior to decisions taken by single executives. But they usually take longer to reach. Or, even if they don't, output per man-hour is usually much lower. Moreover, meetings often require further meetings so that decisions can be explained and people can be briefed on implementing them — and so the costs escalate.

The costs of holding a meeting include not only the pay-rate of the members but also the before-and-after administrative chores:

* Stewart found that informal discussions were especially important, whereas: 'The average time spent in committees was surprisingly small, only 7 per cent.' She also concluded that senior men spend more time in meetings than their juniors. See [8.1].

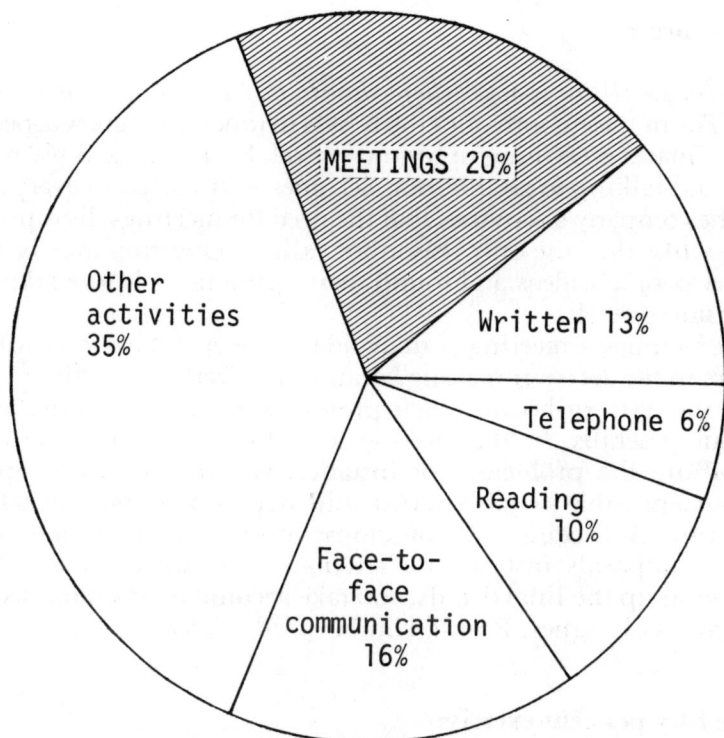

**Figure 13** *This chart shows the average percentage of the working day spent in various activities by managers in a large construction company. Meetings account for about 20 per cent of their time*

drawing up and circulating the notice and agenda; phoning and talking to people; writing letters and lobbying. These are the hidden expenses of holding a meeting, and they push the costs much higher than they first seem.

In fact, the only excuse for the meeting is the anti-meeting — the determined use of some alternative method whenever possible. Call a meeting only when it is the cheapest way of solving the problem. Remember, too, that every manager who attends the meeting has mortgaged a big chunk of his time and so should be certain, before attending, that he has a useful contribution to make.

## Why meet?

*In very small companies there should be little need for meetings at all.* For in these companies the boss is in touch with every aspect and coordinates everything in his own mind. Every day he is seeing people and talking to people, and becomes so involved in every aspect of the company's activities that the need for meetings disappears. In firms like this, the only reason for calling a meeting may be to tap other people's ideas and sound their opinions — before taking the decision oneself.

Sometimes a meeting is unavoidable: people have to be asked to share in the decision-making because of powerful executive or political interests, or because their professional expertise is needed.

But generally, hold a meeting only if there is no cheaper way of handling the problem. For instance, you decide to test opinion about a possible switch to a two-shift system. You consider calling a meeting. But, being cost-conscious, you eventually decide to draft some proposals instead and circulate these for comment. When drawing up the final details, you take account of any remarks made by your colleagues. Result: similar product, lower cost.

## The fifty per cent exercise

The best reforms are those that don't cost money, or actually save it. So why not tackle the cost-benefit problem simply by instructing each company committee to calculate its running costs, then, once it has done this, tell it to hack this figure in half.* After the wails of despair will come the necessary actions: shorter meetings, fewer meetings and the dropping of passengers (committees, like individuals, often run to fat — for which the sovereign remedy is to sweat out some of the adipose). The result is extra thrust at less cost. In my book that's elegant, i.e. the simplest solution to the problem.

Another way of cutting costs is to ask a senior manager to do a sharp-pencil operation on all company committees. Ask him to find the answers to these questions:

1   How much is each committee costing? Where can savings be made?
2   How can committee procedure be streamlined, so saving time and money?

* Financial performance is the least subjective and perhaps the only reliable measure of managerial efficiency.

*Most committees eventually run to fat*

3    Which committees are carrying passengers? Who are they?
4    Could any expensive senior managers on committees be replaced by juniors? Are any senior men sitting on committees that handle low-level problems? (Remember that appointing a junior manager to a committee can provide a valuable kind of executive training.)

Ask the senior manager who is handling this assignment to test out new and simpler procedures in meetings, and to persuade committees to experiment with size and kind of membership until they find the right balance.

## Do you meet too often?

Costs rise astronomically when committees meet *too often*. They may do this because they are told to, or because they feel it is expected of them, or simply because regular meetings may have become a cosy routine. 'We meet for two hours every Friday', a production manager reported. 'I look forward to the meetings. It's a pleasant way of finishing off the week. We always think of something to talk about.' An expensive way of talking shop! Another danger of too-frequent meetings is the apathy and time-wasting that results.

Generally, the most efficient meetings are the *ad hoc* type, called to discuss a specific problem, and disbanded as soon as the problem is solved. The least efficient are meetings of over-played standing committees, which are only held on the basis of reflex or precedent, or as a social occasion.

The *pace* of decision-making is another factor affecting cost. For instance, crash programmes — large groups working to early dead-lines — are costly operations. The more the pace is forced, in fact, the more expensive the decisions, so that a quick and easy way of cutting costs is *(a)* start holding meetings on a problem several weeks or months earlier than you had intended and *(b)* invite fewer people than the number you first thought of. For problems can be solved at the pace that *you* decide, so that it is important to be aware that different rates of progress imply different costs*:

> . . . . fewer people working for longer will always be more productive than more people working faster. This principle is regularly cast aside as the decision-maker needs a quick answer (or thinks he does) and applies the pressure. [8.3]

One reason for the high cost of a crash programme is the disruption of normal work schedules that is usually involved. Yet, a hasty decision is a hasty decision no matter how many people make it.

## Brisker meetings

Study the example of the American company where committee rooms and offices bristle with wall plaques and table ornaments carrying such one-word slogans as 'Now', 'Decide' and 'Act'.

Admittedly, brisker, more urgent sessions are not necessarily the royal road to efficiency, for some problems are more complex than others and take longer to resolve. If a meeting handling a complex problem is short of time it will make a quick decision — and the chances are that it will be a poor one. The National Industrial Conference Board found that a common reason for poor meetings was that the chairman failed to allow the group time to develop its own solution.

One meeting I attended had 15 items crammed onto the agenda. Many of them were important items that would take considerable

---

* 'A project can be performed at a number of different rates, each consistent with the research strategy, but each having a different cost.' See Beattie and Reader [8.2].

time to discuss properly. But we were short of time, and the chairman equated a machine-gun rate of discussion with efficiency. So none of the items was dealt with adequately. Some poor decisions were made that afternoon, among them a decision to buy a piece of land that later turned out to be unsuitable for the purpose it was intended for. None of this would have happened if more time had been available — if, for instance, the fifteen items had been dealt with in three or four separate meetings. The time allowed for a meeting, like the structure of the meeting, should be tailored to the problems on the agenda.

But I'm convinced that most meetings suffer from the opposite problem — too much time and too few decisions. For instance, I've heard of a meeting where four people spent three hours brooding over the best arrangement for keeping the windows clean.

The meeting should be as short as the problem allows. As a gentle incentive to committeemen to keep their meetings crisp and businesslike why not take the following actions?

1  State the duration of the meeting in the memo you sent to members.
2  Impose a time limit on discussion of each item on the agenda.
3  Consider calling the meeting during the last hour of the day. Alternatively, late morning is a good time for brisk meetings because people are more alert then than at other times in the day.
4  During the meeting, don't allow too much side-tracking and

waffling. Don't allow the meeting to degenerate into a social occasion. Frequent summaries are an effective way of keeping the proceedings moving. Summarising has the effect of rounding up one stage of the discussion and leading onto the next.

## Small, informal meetings are cheap and effective

A small, informal meeting is, in many cases, the quickest and cheapest way of dealing with the kind of operational and administrative problems that crop up every day. Imagine, for instance, that you see some operatives standing around smoking in a corner of the factory. You go across to them and discover that they have been waiting about ten minutes for components, and that hold-ups like this are happening three or four times a day. Your first instinct is to call a formal Production meeting for later in the day. But instead you pick up the phone and invite a few people to come to your office there and then to sort the matter out. The advantages of doing it this way are:

1   Calling a small, informal meeting allows operating problems to be cleared up as soon as they arise.
2   Normal working schedules are not disrupted, because only those people who can conveniently attend at that moment will come.
3   There is usually less status-consciousness than in formal meetings, so that senior staff have to do their share of the listening — which is a valuable effect when production problems are being discussed.
4   The costs of running small, informal meetings are minimal.
5   The manager who calls the meeting has the great advantage of being able to hold the meeting in his own office, and with the people that only he thinks should be there.

Claude Riviere has described a Japanese company which has scrapped formal meetings and instead holds informal stand-up meetings of all management staff three times a week [8.4]. The room in which the meetings are held has only one table and a few chairs. Coffee is served as people move from group to group discussing day-to-day problems. These short, informal get-togethers are opportunities to see, to hear and to overhear: that is why the company is convinced that they are more productive than formal management meetings. The meetings are held in the last half-hour of the afternoon so that the ordinary work schedules are not disrupted: in fact, the managers probably get through *more* work in the week because, instead of sending memos or ringing people about a problem, it can be saved for the coffee conference.

**Value for money?**

How much value for money are you getting from company committees? What are their weaknesses and strengths and where could improvements be made? To find the answers to these questions, why not ask each committee to complete the rating scale shown in Table 3 and then discuss the results?

An alternative form of self-diagnosis is for each committee to submit a written report of its work — and results — to top management every year. Ask the committee to include comments on such matters as *Size* (should the committee be smaller or larger?); *Membership* (are any changes needed?); *Attendance* (average, and by each member); *Committee objectives* (were they achieved?); *Were committee decisions well implemented?* (If not, analyse the reasons).

Or, after a meeting, you could simply ask the participants what they thought of it. You could do this informally, by calling into their offices and chatting about the meeting; or systematically, by means of a confidential questionnaire with such headings as:

1   Are you always clear about the objectives of meetings?
2   Do you get adequate background information about important issues?
3   Are you pleased with the way that meetings are run?
4   Are good decisions always made? If not, why not?
5   How could meetings be made more efficient?

Use the information gained from exercises like these to plan reforms to boost the efficiency of meetings.

**Gadgetry**

Another way of reducing costs in the long run is to make greater use of modern communications equipment. For instance, *an internal telephone link-up* is available which allows up to ten people to talk together in snap conferences without any of the participants needing to leave his desk. Daily work schedules are not disrupted, nobody wastes time hanging around and waiting for others to appear, and preparation is minimal.

**Table 3**

| Effective                          OR | Ineffective |
|---|---|
| **1 Efficiency** | |
| Committee thinks straight and logically. Clear sense of direction and progress in meetings. Good decisions. | Lack of direction in meetings. Much waffling and side-tracking. Poor decisions frequently made. |
| **2 Human resources** | |
| Equal participation. Full use of talents of all members. | Unequal participation. Little use made of talents and experience of some members. |
| **3 Communication** | |
| Full and free communication between members in meetings. Mutual trust among members. | Guarded, cautious communication in meetings. Mutual suspicion. |
| **4 Discipline** | |
| Controls, and sometimes procedure, self-imposed. Free and tolerant atmosphere. | Controls imposed. Restrictive atmosphere. Conformist pressures. |
| **5 Conflict** | |
| Acceptance and working through of conflict. | Avoidance of conflict through suppression and too-easy compromise. |
| **6 Team spirit** | |
| General concern for each other and the group. Commitment to group goals. | Self-seeking. Pursuit of individual or sectional goals. |

In the Jim Walter Corporation, a large American construction company, divisional managers at all levels use *teletype meetings* to keep in touch with each other's plans and performance. For instance, every Saturday morning executives in the home building division have a teletype conference to review the week's orders with the regional managers. Each manager can see instantly how his own results compare with his colleagues', who may be thousands of miles away.

In Britain, the GPO's *Confravision Service* allows businessmen to confer at long distance cheaply and easily by providing sound and vision links between groups of people in different cities. There should be a nationwide network of confravision studios by the 1980s. No longer need overworked executives trail their weary bones up and down the country to hold meetings in alien cities.

*Closed-circuit television* can be much quicker and cheaper than staging live meetings or conferences. Sun Oil used CCTV to introduce a new brand of petrol to dealers, distributors and employees throughout the country instead of holding a string of expensive dealer meetings, and saved more than £100,000. Ford use TV to take their new cars and tractors to their overseas managers instead of calling these managers to attend high-cost meetings in Detroit or Dagenham.

CCTV can deliver your chairman, with his special brand of persuasion, right to the people he needs to convince. It even offers world-wide coverage for the multinational corporation. More than a thousand persons in America, Japan, Britain and Australia participated in the official opening ceremony of the Mount Newman iron ore project in western Australia. The operation, made possible by the communication satellite system, was expensive — but still much cheaper than flying hundreds of people to the function.

**Fun meetings**

Cut running costs indirectly by taking positive actions to boost members' enthusiasm and morale — and therefore their productivity. For instance, you can add a vital interest to meetings by varying the times and formats of meetings. When the committee is wrestling with an exciting issue, why not call meetings once a week instead of once a month and so give members a sense of pace and achievement?

Why not hold a fun meeting occasionally — a theatre trip; a brainstorming session in a pub; a visit to another company or geographical area with which the committee is concerned?

One German company boosts the efficiency of meetings by exposing committees to each others' criticism or acclaim. Occasional joint meetings are held and attended by *all* company committees. During these sessions, the committees hear about each other's work — and results — in detail. Then comments are invited.

Another way of introducing the competitive element is to give points to each committee at quarterly intervals according to how

*Hold a fun meeting occasionally*

successfully they have controlled budgets, solved problems, made breakthroughs of various kinds, achieved their objectives. Thus a kind of league table is created with each committee fighting for the championship. The achievements of the league leaders can be publicised in the house magazine or in special news sheets, and mentioned in the annual report. Not only would those E for Excellence flags be proudly worn by the winners but, more important, they would encourage the other committees to win flags of their own.

Managers are often judged on their ability to cut costs and control budgets. The resulting competition among plants and departments creates an internal tension that keeps operations lean and efficient. So what's wrong with applying the same competitive principle to all those fat committees?

Meetings are an expensive activity and should be held only if there is no cheaper way of solving the problem. To justify high running costs, efficiency of operation is essential. Cost efficiency can be inproved by instructing committees to slash their running costs, by expelling passengers, by replacing senior men with juniors and by introducing the competitive element into committee operations. Often the simplest method of all for boosting efficiency is to slap a time limit on meetings.

*Improving a committee's performance depends largely on making an accurate diagnosis of its ailments, followed by suitable treatment. This chapter outlines some diagnostic methods, describes some common complaints and gives hints for treating them.*

# 9

# Some common ailments

Meetings consume time and money yet fail to produce good results. This was one of the conclusions reached by the Ansul Chemical Company when it took a critical look at how its meetings were working. The other conclusions were:

1 Often the wrong people attend.
2 Often meetings are slowly and badly run.
3 The consensus-seeking machinery of meetings reduces policy to the common denominator and results in dreary decision-making.
4 Committees are often no more than an organised pooling of ignorance.

Most of us, thinking of the meetings we attend, could easily add to the list:

5 Meetings breed compromise solutions that nobody really supports.
6 Meetings can be a cul-de-sac into which ideas are lured and then quietly strangled.

And so on.

## Officialitis

The disadvantages and inefficiencies seem to be particularly numerous in the public service area — perhaps because, generally, there is even less pressure than in most companies to get value for money. Hence, many local government committees seem to meet simply to endorse decisions already taken in their names by senior officials — an expensive kind of rubber-stamp operation.*

Some committees in the public sector are emasculated because of an official who manipulates the committee for his own administrative purposes. As Wheare has pointed out [9.1], the committee may become the official's instrument; he reads its letters and writes its replies ('The committee require me to point out that . . .'), yet he is really expressing his own ideas and making his own decisions:

> He holds up the committee as a vague body which would be 'reluctant' to do this or would by 'unhappy' about that; a body which 'had not contemplated acting on these lines' . . . . In this way citizens are held back from the committee . . . so as to avoid holding up the administrative processes that the official is carrying out. [9.1]

Not many officials are as scrupulous in approach as the secretary of a committee set up in 1874 to choose a design for the chapel of an Oxford college, who wrote:

> 'When the committee laid the plans before the G(overning) B(ody) the GB did not accept any of them, but the reasons given were very various . . . . It seems then to the committee that they are not in a position to give such an answer to Sir G.G. Scott as might be taken to represent the opinion of the GB.' [9.2]

I suppose that the short answer to this particular problem is to crack the whip and tame the official — who is, after all, only the servant of a servant.†

## No sense of direction

Here is an example of how a meeting's decisions may be good in themselves, so to speak, but ultimately damaging because they cut

* In Britain, *The Local Government Act, 1972*, empowers Councils to delegate almost any of their powers to officials.

† 'The notion of a committee carries with it the idea of a body being in some manner or degree responsible or subordinate or answerable in the last report to the body or person who set it up . . . There is inherent in the notion of a committee some idea of a derived or secondary or dependent status . . . It acts on behalf of or with responsibility to another body.' [9.3]

across or fail to support company strategy. A small instrument company, which sold most of its products by direct mail, had a policy of fast service and low prices, achieved by cutting costs to the bone. When this firm merged with a large electronics company, a meeting of senior managers was called and two decisions were taken:

1    To appoint salesmen to sell the instruments to the retail trade. 'Every firm needs personal sales representation', one of the electronics managers declared.
2    To set up a more sophisticated accounting system (involving considerable capital expenditure) in the instruments division.

Looked at in the abstract, both were perfectly sound decisions and based on valid premises. But look at them *in context*. Both decisions cut clean across the instrument company's strategy for survival. Later events showed just *how* wrong the decisions were, for they led to increased costs, increased prices — and a consequent slump in sales.

Perhaps the most telling measure of a meeting's success is the extent to which its work contributed to overall company strategy. This raises the problem of how to assess committee effectiveness in the absence of any coherent corporate strategy — or when nobody knows what it is. A recent study reveals that a high proportion of companies lack a sense of strategic direction and that this has the effect of making these companies less competitive:

> Those companies that could not agree as to corporate direction, could not define responsibility for decision-making, nor were likely to identify changes in the trading environment. [9.4]

In firms without a clear strategy, it seems, trading opportunities and warning signals alike are bound to be missed. Moreover, you can never be sure that the people who are taking decisions in meetings are the people who *should* be taking them. *Or that the decisions taken are actually in the interests of the company.*

Corporate strategy is the rock on which particular management meetings should build. But in many firms, strategy formation is

> highly diffuse and political in nature ... with the personal goals and departmental affiliations of ... members affecting the directions in which they wish to move the organisation. [9.5]

How often could ineffective meetings and poor decisions be explained by the board of directors' neglecting to formulate (then publicise) a clear strategy for the company? Or by participants in meetings ignoring *company* strategy and persuing departmental or personal goals?

The moral is, I suppose, to create administrative controls to ensure that company strategy is publicised and that it is followed in meetings.


## Total loss of control

In a company that manufactured industrial gas appliances, a senior manager was asked to assess the performance of the progress committee, which met once every three to four weeks. The first thing that the manager noticed was that no notice or agenda was sent to members, who were informed of meetings orally — usually over the telephone. So usually at least one person failed to get the message and consequently did not attend the meeting.

Most members had no prior knowledge of the objectives of any particular meeting and, since no working papers were ever circulated, they arrived at meetings totally unprepared to take decisions. The discussion was usually monopolised by the three senior engineers who knew in advance what the meeting would be discussing and who had the chance to brief themselves.

No records of meetings were kept and often people forgot to carry out actions agreed in meetings.

After attending three meetings, the manager made a diagnosis, submitted in the form of a written report to the Production Director. These were the problems he listed:

1   Lack of planning.
2   Lack of information.
3   Ill-defined objectives.
4   Uneven contributions.
5   Low-quality decisions (because not enough people contributed to them).

To overcome these weaknesses the manager suggested the following reforms:

1   A short preliminary meeting should be held to enable the members to agree on objectives, an agenda and any special procedure required.
2   Notice and agenda to be pre-circulated three or four days before the meeting together with a brief statement of objectives and brief factual background information.
3   The chairman should make a point of drawing junior members into the discussion.

4    One member should act as secretary and take an action set of minutes for circulation immediately after the meeting. These would remind individuals of any actions required before the next meeting.

The need for these simple reforms was perfectly clear to the manager — the outside observer — but not to the members themselves. As a result of the reforms that followed his intervention meetings became far more businesslike, more people became involved in the discussions, and more ground was covered in less time.

The simple expedient of asking a senior manager to attend meetings as an observer and to suggest possible reforms led to a tremendous boost in this committee's operating efficiency.

### Dead but won't lie down

Sometimes a committee becomes institutionalised and continues to meet long after its original purpose is achieved. Once I was a member of a committee set up by a local organisation to raise funds. We used to meet on Friday nights in a pub. The funds were duly raised — but we carried on meeting in the pub because we wanted to. This meant thinking up some problems to solve, so we discussed public relations. Then the decline in membership. Then several other issues. None of our recommendations was ever carried out, but that wasn't the point.

Many company committees also keep going for similar reasons, long after their usefulness has ended. They're dead but they won't lie down. That is why every standing committee in the organisation should be assessed by a senior manager at least once every two years. This kind of surveillance is needed because in the fast-changing world of industry committees can rapidly become obsolete.

Unless the company makes sure that its major standing committees are effective, it may find itself manipulated by groups of senior managers who conspire together to get a strangle-hold on decision-making. That is why, at least once every two years, the organisation should review its entire committee structure, assessing each committee's strengths and weaknesses and making sure that it is still contributing to corporate goals. Some assessment methods are described below.

*1   Sit in on meetings and tape the proceedings for later playback and analysis.* (Events are happening so fast that many of them are lost using any other method.) Better still, use videotape to record and retrieve the key points of the meeting for later analysis: the members forget that the camera is there after five or ten minutes. This will allow you to study non-verbal behaviour — gestures, facial expressions, and so on — which may hold the clues to many kinds of inefficiency.

*2   Assess whether or not a committee is regularly meeting its objectives.* Do the chairman and the members of the committee feel that objectives are being achieved? Are they always clear about exactly what the objectives *are?* Remember that uncertainty about objectives leads to lack of direction in meetings and to irrelevant decisions. Has the committee got *long-term objectives?* If so, does it hold to them, and is it achieving them?

*3   Judge if a committee is being forced to rubber-stamp somebody else's decisions.* If so, who benefits most from this arrangement — the company or some senior executive who is using meetings simply to add respectability to his solo decisions? (In the public sector, too, important decisions are frequently taken far from the apparent decision-point: for instance, by a political party weeks or months before the local government committee meeting takes place which, ostensibly, is to take the decision.)

*4   Study the actions and changes brought about by committee decisions.* Was the meeting successful in leading to new business, savings, technological or marketing breakthroughs? This approach assumes that the decisions were good if the outcomes were good. Of course, good decisions may not work out in practice because of circumstances beyond the control of the members. For instance, I was once involved in planning a promising advertising campaign which was jettisoned at the last minute because of a change in the law.

If apparently good decisions are not working out in practice is this because of lack of political sensitivity in members? For example, radical decisions being taken within a conservative company; not sensing that the decision would be unacceptable to certain groups or to powerful individuals, etc. Or does it simply indicate that meetings are being used by certain executives as a way of avoiding taking action — that decisions are not *meant* to be implemented and that meetings are being used as a delaying tactic?

A clear answer is needed to questions like these because it will tell you the kind of reforms that are needed to boost operating efficiency.

## Better meetings by training

A committee of top-level executives can cost thousands of pounds a year to run. Yet how many companies will spend even extra hundreds to eliminate maladies such as those described above? (On the contrary, as soon as earnings come under pressure, training budgets are always among the first to be slashed.)

When meetings are in poor health the responsibility for revitalising them surely lies with top management. The Board of Ansul Chemicals, for instance, accepted this responsibility after discovering how inefficiently company meetings were working, and trained its executives in the formal aspects of committee work and in dealing with the psychological factors. Dramatic improvements followed with meetings getting more accomplished in the same time. In Britain the Central Electricity Generating Board, British Oxygen and ICI are among the very few companies that have provided similar kinds of training for their executives. Yet how can people be expected to contribute forcefully and wisely to committee work *without* adequate training?

> Is it fair to expect anyone to be effective and forthright on a Regional Hspital Board or a local authority planning committee if he or she doesn't understand the system in which they are playing such an important role? Millions of pounds and thousands of lives may be affected by a single decision. Yet these representatives are expected to acquire insight and understanding in the most haphazard fashion . . . For the most part our representatives are being educated on the job — an educational method that industry has abandoned because it perpetuates mistakes, is inefficient and ultimately counter-productive.

The writer is explaining the problem of members of committees in the public sector. But people who attend company meetings have precisely the same problem — how to make a forceful contribution and make sound decisions without training.

For instance, role-playing is a simple but invaluable training method for committeemen. For when they role-play the union boss, the angry customer, the head of a rival department, they begin to experience how these people feel and think. Thus a new kind of sympathy and understanding is created so that future communication is more fruitful. According to the National Training Laboratory, role playing exercises should have the following qualities:

1   The scenes played should deal with valid problems in human relations.
2   The problem should be clear, single and specific.
3   The problem should be such that the trainees can understand how the characters actually feel.
4   The problem should mean something to the players and to any observers.

## Sensitivity training

Often meetings are wrecked by too much conflict or by various kinds of irrational behaviour; and when this is the case T-Group training can lead to great improvements. T-Group and other forms of sensitivity training can give individuals insights into their own attitudes and behaviour that they would never have got otherwise, and help them over humps in personal development. When they are exposed to 'Feedback' they learn about the impact they are having on other people and make necessary adjustments.

Even very simple feedback exercises can make a big impact. For example, trainees are asked to discuss some controversial subject. They quickly split into opposed camps. Conflict erupts. At this point the trainer interrupts the discussion and asks each side to state the other side's point of view to the other side's satisfaction. Participants quickly learn how fiercely they have distorted each other's arguments, intentions and motives, and so learn to listen to others in meetings more carefully.

Bunker described lasting behaviour changes as a result of T-Group training, including (a) more effort to understand and listen to others, (b) more tact and tolerance, (c) less willingness to make snap judgements.

Sensitivity training, however, needs to be handled by reputable experts (in the United Kingdom, the T-Groups run by the Tavistock Institute and by Leeds University have won a high reputation), and a careful selection procedure is needed to screen out individuals who could be damaged by the experience. One hears stories of people who committed suicide while on T-Group courses. One of the trainees on a course that I attended was so disturbed by the experience that he spent the whole night wandering the streets.

## The practice method

Another useful exercise is to hold a training meeting on a controversial subject, tape the proceedings, then play the tape back to the trainees immediately afterwards. They are surprised when they hear how crudely they cut each other off, interrupt in mid-sentence, abuse and shout at each other and refuse to listen.

A way of dealing with a large group of trainees is to split them into sub-groups and run several training meetings simultaneously, with a change of chairman in each meeting every ten or fifteen minutes. Thus in a short period of time, every man has the chance to practise his chairmanship and gets the benefit of hearing the group's assessment of his performance.

By far the best way of becoming a better chairman or a better committeeman is to *practise* being one — if possible, with immediate feedback on your efforts. Committeemen — indeed, whole committees — become strong by wrestling with actual problems (then assessing how well they coped with them). And they learn as much from failure as from success, because success only makes them feel good, but failure makes them analyse the *reasons* for failing. That is why training-by-practice is such an effective method. By contrast, traditional one-way training methods such as reading and listening to lectures, have little effect on *performance*.

But unless trainees are given the opportunity to *apply* what they learn in training sessions they quickly become stifled by the bad old ways that made training necessary in the first place. How useful are Theory Y assumptions in a Theory X organisation?

## A diagnostic checklist

Use this checklist to reveal sore-spots in meetings that require corrective action:
- are members always clear about *objectives?*
- Does the *chairman* dominate meetings? (This leads to one-man decision-making.)
- Are members always provided with *adequate background information?*
- Is there *equal participation* in meetings? Are the human resources being fully utilised?
- Is there too much *waffling and side-tracking* in meetings? (If so, committee procedure may need to be tightened up,

or the chairman may have to be replaced.)
— Is there evidence of *unresolved emotional problems,* e.g.
  much conflict, or withdrawal symptoms by some members? If so, would a change of membership help matters?
  Would some form of sensitivity training help members to
  overcome these problems?
—   *Do meetings drag on too long?* If so, would it help to
  impose a time-limit on meetings?
— *Are the right people being invited to meetings?* (See Chapter 10.)
— *Are good decisions made?* If not, would it be practicable to
  train at least the chairman in problem-solving techniques? (See Chapter 5).
— *Are decisions being well implemented?* If not, is this
  because of incompetence by the meeting organiser? Or
  because people affected by decisions are not being consulted in advance?
— *Do the meeting's decisions contribute to overall company
  strategy?* If not, is this because of the pursuit of departmental or individual goals; or because members are uncertain
  of what company strategy *is?*

Improving a committee's performance depends largely on making an accurate diagnosis of its ailments followed by suitable treatment. Usually the participants themselves are so involved in the
proceedings that they are unable to sit back and make an objective
assessment of what is going on and where improvements are
needed. This explains the value of using a disinterested observer to
estimate performance and make recommendations for reform. In
the long run, though, a raising of standards depends more on the
provision of suitable training for committeemen — and on the members themselves accepting the need for change.

Africans, like Arabs, often prefer to sit close together in meetings

But Englishmen, Scandinavians and North Americans dislike touching and generally feel uncomfortable when sitting very close to other participants

Thus a meeting between African and English businessmen, say, can be an uncomfortable experience for all the participants. One way of cooling the encounter is to take special care with the seating arrangements

During meetings of this kind cross-cultural variations can lead to misunderstandings. For instance, when African participants laugh they may be expressing embarrassment or surprise, not amusement. Not realising this, the European members may pursue the subject instead of dropping it

Different cultures use different cues (glances, looking away, coughing, etc.) for controlling the listening-speaking sequence. Thus 'meshing' is often poor, i.e. there is no flow in the discussion; or there are many embarrassing pauses; or everybody tries to speak at once

Arabs often prefer the head-on position in meetings, and they look at the person they are speaking to with great intensity. But the European members may interpret this as an aggressive challenge

**Figure 14   When different nationalities meet** — *Meetings between businessmen from different countries can easily lead to misunderstanding or resentment because different nationalities have different preferences and codes of behaviour. But the spread of multi-national corporations and the growth of international trade means that businessmen are spending more and more time in meet-*

The person most spoken to and most frequently looked at by the other participants is probably (a) the best-liked or (b) the most powerful individual in the meeting

Leaning forward in the meeting shows interest, leaning back may be a sign of boredom or unconcern

Looking away while speaking signals a lack of self-confidence or uncertainty about what is being said

Finger or foot-tapping is a sure sign of emotional arousal. So is a high blinking-rate

Research evidence suggests that when people appear in meetings wearing spectacles this adds, on average, about 13 points to their judged IQs

**Figure 15  Body language** —*the ability to read basic body-language in meetings helps you to stay in control of the discussion by telling you what the other participants are feeling and thinking*

*The term "breakdown in communications"*
*is the currently fashionable way of avoiding*
*saying what is wrong.*

**Antony Jay**

# Part 2
# PLANNING AND CONTROL

*Packing a meeting with top-level talent can be an expensive way of getting poor decisions made. Operational and day-to-day administrative problems, for instance, are best handled by people from lower managerial levels. It pays to push decision-making as far down the organisation as it will go. Another principle to observe is making sure that all departments that will be affected by a decision are involved in the discussions — through representatives — from an early stage.*

# 10
# Who to invite

Beware of inviting people to meetings simply because of their high status in the organisation. For one of the secrets of managing meetings efficiently is to push decision-making as far down the organisation as it will go, i.e. to the lowest level competent to handle the problem. This is based on the sound management principle of getting a good job done at the lowest possible cost.

The presence of high status individuals at a meeting can actually be counter-productive because they tend to dominate proceedings whether or not they understand the problem, and to have an undue influence on the decision-making. Torrance (1954) found that high-status participants are more successful in getting their ideas accepted even when they are wrong.

Packing a committee with top talent doesn't guarantee good decisions. This was the conclusion reached by Carl Blumenthal, Chairman of the Bendix Corporation, after attending hundreds of meetings at many different levels:

I had thought that the higher up you go the more sensible the decisions that are made. I found that it ain't necessarily so . . . . When issues get confused on the way to the top the chance for wise decisions is less than it might have been at lower levels.

Lower-level meetings, Blumenthal implies, make better decisions on some issues than meetings of senior managers.

Why, for instance, call a meeting of senior managers to decide how to break through a manufacturing bottleneck or to resolve some other operating problem when a meeting of junior managers or supervisors is more competent to handle the problem? For the further removed a committee is from actual operations, the less valid its interpretation of the problem. *Perhaps top-level meetings should be reserved for general policy decisions and for long-term decisions in general, such as which of three possible locations would form the best site for a new plant; or an assessment of ideas for new product lines.*

## Invite from the appropriate levels

One of the basic skills of managing meetings is to invite people from the levels most appropriate to deal with the problem. Generally, the level should vary according to the time-span of the decisions to be made:

1   *Long-term strategic decisions,* e.g. whether to diversify or whether to commit the company to new markets. These should be made at meetings of senior managers, because only senior men would have the experience and the over-view to grasp the financial implications of a particular decision and to overcome the inherent uncertainty of this kind of long-term decision-making. An essential preparatory move when organising this kind of meeting is to pump relevant information up to the top-level membership.

2   *Medium-term managerial decisions,* e.g. which kind of machinery to purchase or, the re-structuring of a department. Decisions of this kind should be made at meetings of middle managers — perhaps with a senior man in the chair — for they involve less uncertainty and risk. Less is at stake, as far as the company is concerned. More attention to technical or administrative detail is required; but also an appreciation of the implications for the company of any decisions that are taken.

*Top-level meetings shouldn't be making low-level decisions*

3 *Day-to-day operating decisions*, e.g. how to deal with a discipline problem or how to smooth out a specific crimp in production. These decisions should be made at meetings of supervisors or junior managers because only people of this level have the detailed administrative or technical know-how needed to deal with the problem. The action required from the meeting organiser is almost the reverse of that needed for top-level meetings, i.e. to pump the decision-point down to where most of the necessary information and know-how is concentrated.

So when deciding who to invite to a meeting, be clear about the kind of decisions that will be required — then invite people from the appropriate levels. And never include problems with different time-spans on the same agenda, because then there are bound to be some items that the members will not be able to deal with adequately.

Often people from a lower level are best qualified to make the decision, although financial or other factors may require that a follow-up meeting is held so that a higher level can approve or ratify it.

If a decision affects a single activity or department it should be left to the head of that department or function: involving people at higher levels only reduces efficiency and damages discipline.

*Diverse membership may lead to flying fur and feathers*

When people from an inappropriate level or function are invited to a meeting poor decisions are the likely result. A meeting of middle managers which, by some mistake, is asked to make a major policy decision can hardly be expected to take into account all the various factors involved or to understand the full implications to the company of any decision taken, simply because they lack the necessary breadth of experience.

When low-level meetings are given high-level problems to solve Parkinson's Law of Triviality tends to operate: time spent in making the decision is inversely proportional to its importance. I've heard of £50,000 being voted for a new project after ten minutes' brisk opinion-giving. And I'm ashamed to admit that I once took part in a meeting that decided where to site a new coffee machine only after ninety minutes' solemn discussion!

## Technical experts

Complicated technical problems should, of course, be solved by the appropriate technical specialists, and the nature of the problem itself tells you who to invite to the meeting — a manufacturing problem requires production personnel, and so on. But you have to think more carefully about the invitation list when the problem, although a 'technical' one, requires a team of specialists from different functions, e.g. a systems design job or a new product design. Here the trick is to identify (and, if necessary, take advice about), the different skills and functions that will be required and to make sure that they are all represented at the meeting.

*Apparently straightforward technical problems that can easily be taken by the appropriate experts, may have a big 'impact' and affect many other parts of the organisation. For instance, a new production schedule can effect not only Manufacturing but also Personnel, Sales, Marketing, the Management Accountants' department and so on. So be clear about which other parts of the organisation will be affected by the decision and make sure that you involve all these other departments in the discussions from an early stage.*

In this way you can avoid backlash and resistance *after* the decision has been taken by involving them *in* the decision-making. Involve these departments either by inviting representatives to the meetings; or, if this would make the meetings uncomfortably large, through liaison with the chairman.

Certain open-ended problems, such as how to improve in-plant labour relations or how to improve the company image, are best tackled by groups of people of widely varying talents and experience rather than by the appropriate like-minded experts. This is precisely because the problems *are* open-ended: not even the experts (which experts?) know the answers. There are no formulae. The problems need to be solved 'creatively'.

So to deal with problems of this kind, why not invite people from different departments and different levels of the organisation to attend the meeting? Think of each member as possessing one piece of an extremely complex puzzle: if you can assemble *all* the different pieces required you may get a solution. Admittedly, one of the risks of a diverse membership is that — particularly in the first meeting — there will be a true non-meeting of minds and flying fur and feathers because of fights between the different functions. But very quickly they all begin to understand one another's languages, to pool their knowledge and to build on one another's ideas.

Whenever a number of departments or units have to be represented at a meeting, make sure that the people you invite accurately represent opinion in their units — or at least know what it is.

## The advantages of diverse membership

Hoffman and Maier (1961) found that meetings made up of people of unlike personality often produce better solutions than like-minded groups. The reason may be the wide range of ideas that is likely; or simply that different-minded people tend to disagree and this prevents over-hasty decisions being made. Broadly similar conclusions were reached by Pelz (1956) who found that optimum performance comes from consulting colleagues whose orientation differs from one's own (and who therefore test and challenge one's ideas), and also consulting colleagues who share one's approach (and who therefore support and develop one's ideas). (Perhaps this is one of the reasons for the efficiency of the jury system.)

In one experiment, military personnel were given problems to solve. Groups whose members initially disagreed about the best course of action produced better decisions in the end than groups where agreement was high throughout.

One manager told me that he believes passionately in meetings for men only. No mere MCP, the manager has reached this conclusion reluctantly, after more than twenty years' hard experience. According to him, mixed-sex groups split into cliques, are often disrupted by incredibly fierce in-fighting and, when they are not fighting, waste a lot of time on irrelevant chat. Freud decided, more than half a century ago, that same-sex groups cohere while mixed groups disintegrate, because of innate psychological factors. More recent investigations by Scott, Gurnee and others, suggest that single-sex committees work more efficiently than mixed. The practical implication, I suppose, is to be aware of a possible problem if drawing up a mixed-sex invitation list and to think of ways of solving it, if necessary, during the meeting.

Incidentally, committee cliques — men *v.* women, young *v.* old, radicals *v.* conservatives, etc. — can have disastrous results on productivity in meetings. They generate conflict and contradictory goals so that the committee as a whole lacks direction and a clear, unambiguous policy. A quick and easy way of breaking up cliques is by changing the membership. For instance, you could replace the clique leaders by more conciliatory types.

## Membership shake-up

A shake-up of membership is also the sovereign remedy for another common ailment, the seriously lowered metabolism that seems to affect many standing committees. The symptoms are easy to recognise:

1   The committee's thinking is stale and unimaginative.
2   Too-easy compromises are made in meetings because of a general lack of commitment, and this results in poor decisions being made.
3   The committee can only handle certain kinds of problem — usually the kind it has handled in the past.
4   Members produce stereotyped solutions. Their approach is rather like that of a burnt-out lecturer teaching a subject by rote.

## Placing people in committees

The ability to place people in committees is an important executive skill. It involves:

1   The ability to analyse the types of problems for discussion and to decide what kind of people will be needed to solve them. A problem requiring analytical ability will need a different sort of membership from 'creative' problem-solving, where imagination and 'divergent' thinking are the main requirements.
2   The ability to assess people's present and potential abilities with objectivity.
3   Refusing to invite people to meetings simply because they are on the old-boy network, or because they 'talk well', i.e. glibly and loudly.
4   Recognising what the 'time-span' of any decision will be, then inviting people from the appropriate level.

When a meeting is being called to take a very important decision — one that will affect the whole future of the company and the security of its employees — it should be given super staff support: very senior and experienced managers who can think out agendas and have enough energy and leverage to get any decisions carried out smoothly. A meeting of this kind can be sparked by guest appearances. The opinions of the company chairman, say, who is only seen on red letter days, can carry great weight and impress participants with the gravity of a situation or the desirability of a certain course of action.

## Choosing the chairman

One way of boosting the performance of a committee is to appoint a forceful and experienced manager as a temporary chairman. Then, once the committee is working well, replace him with a promising junior. This releases the senior man for top-level executive activity; develops the junior for higher responsibility; acts like an adrenalin shot on the committee.

Set a new committee rolling by first appointing the chairman and asking him to select his own membership. No doubt he'll choose people with whom he already has good working relationships. And so politics in the new committee will be kept to a minimum. Right from the start, the chairman and members will have mutual trust and confidence in each other — an important characteristic of effective meetings. The importance of mutual trust among members has been underlined by Schein:

> Case evidence has shown that if a group is composed of members who trust one another and have learned to work well together, it can work more quickly and efficiently than any member alone. [10.1]

Gibb reaches the same conclusion:

> With low trust, people use more strategy, filter information, build inter-personal facades, camouflage attitudes, deliberately or unconsciously hold back relevant feelings and information in the process of inter-personal in-fighting, distort feedback — and thus indirectly sabotage productivity. [10.2]

Negative behaviour of this kind can be avoided by asking the *chairman* to select the members of a committee. *So why not go a step further and ask him — or the entire committee — to select its own problems to solve, on the principle that people know what they are good at?*

An alternative approach, also aimed at improving group process in meetings, would be to ask a newly formed committee to select its own chairman. In any newly formed group, the 'natural' leaders (for that particular group) quickly emerge, and the others in the group know exactly who they are.

A committee that elects its own chairman, or which is selected by him, is likely to possess another important characteristic of effective groups — a membership which is attracted to and loyal to the leader and which strives to achieve group objectives. In *New Patterns of Management*, Likert lists twenty-four characteristics of highly effective groups, including the one mentioned here.

**Don't promote the 'star'**

Often the man appointed as chairman is the committee's star per-
former — sometimes with disappointing results. His new role
forces him to be a coordinator and conciliator and to suppress his
own ideas — his greatest asset. Alternatively, his ideas burst
through in meetings irrepressibly so that he remains a brilliant con-
tributor but fails as a chairman. If a man is making an outstanding
contribution as an ordinary member of a committee, think carefully
before forcing him to change his role.

A man whose role does need to be changed is the awkward, aggressive individual; the super-pessimist who, in meetings, spends his
time pouring scorn on other people's ideas and producing a thousand reasons why he thinks their proposals are unworkable. Often
this kind of person becomes an effective chairman because he is
strong enough for the job. (This is an important qualification
because every chairman is tested by the group to see if he is strong
enough to control them, and if he fails the test the committee will
never work efficiently until he is replaced.) Moreover, his new role
forces him to think in terms of conciliation and winning cooperation so that for the first time he has to use his abundant energies
positively and constructively.

**Who to invite**

Packing meetings with top talent is no guarantee that good decisions will be made. Long-term strategic decisions require top-level
meetings, but day-to-day operating decisions are much better understood by lower managerial levels. Thus it literally pays to push decision-making down to the lowest level competent to handle the
problem. On the other hand, it is often pointed out that you can
push decision-making down but it won't stay down:

> Although the lower levels are constantly crying out
> for . . . freedom of action . . . they are often reluctant to exercise
> such freedom of action when it is given to them. They try hard
> to involve the upper levels as much as possible, hoping by secur-
> ing 'approval' or 'concurrence' before they act to shield them-
> selves from total blame for the consequences of their actions.
> [10.3]

When a decision will affect other departments, involve these in
the discussions from an early stage — either through direct represen-

tation at the meetings or by liasion with the chairman. Thus these other parts of the organisation become involved in the decision-making and their cooperation in implementing any decisions is ensured.

Invite the appropriate experts to meetings making technical decisions, but remember that openended problems (How shall we improve turnover?) are best tackled by a group of people drawn from different departments and functions. One experiment suggests that when people in a meeting initially disagree they generally produce better decisions in the end than do like-minded people who agree throughout.

When a committee becomes stale and unimaginative the quickest remedy is a membership shake-up. This action also overcomes the problem of cliques.

A competent outside observer who sits in on company meetings will soon be able to advise you about any membership changes that are needed to boost efficiency, and about which members would make effective chairmen. The choice of chairman is crucial. To be certain that the right man is appointed, why not first appoint the members of the committee then ask them to select their own chairman. Invariably, they select one of the 'natural' leaders (for that particular committee) who quickly emerge in any group. The reverse approach is equally effective: appoint a tough and resourceful individual as chairman and invite him to select his own members. These will be people with whom he already has a good working relationship, and so 'process problems' in meetings are likely to be minimal.

*A meeting should be big enough to possess the human resources needed for solving the problem, but small enough to avoid serious problems in both organisation and communication. But there is no optimum size for all purposes and all committees. The quickest and easiest way of discovering the right balance for a particular committee is trial and error. For many purposes, though, meetings of between five and nine members seem to work well.*

# 11
# Size

A well-trained committee can be the hottest horse in the manager's stable, but only if it's carrying the right weight. Meetings that are too large or too small don't work well, although the precise number of members should, of course, be based on a knowledge of the subject for discussion, of the people concerned, and on other local factors.

Small meetings reach agreement more quickly than large ones and the members tend to work harder — perhaps because they have a greater chance to influence the outcome, or simply because poor contributors are conspicuous in small groups. According to Argyle and his colleagues, some tasks, such as drafting or fact-finding, are always best performed by small meetings [11.1].

But in small meetings there is, obviously, more risk of freak decisions because the error-correcting properties of large groups are missing. Very small meetings of five or less are often more concerned with maintaining good relationships among members than with thrashing out the problem.

Large meetings are *potentially* more effective simply because they possess a bigger fund of resources: the bigger the meeting the greater the chance that it contains somebody who can solve the problem. But in practice, large meetings suffer from 'process losses', i.e. communication problems and lack of coordination. For instance, in large groups, most contributions tend to be directed at a single high-status individual and the advantages of free interaction are lost. The larger the group the greater the difficulty it has in becoming an effective and cohesive unit.

Here are some of the characteristic maladies of large meetings:

Lack of coordination
Lack of control
Poor use of time
Difficulty in achieving a consensus
The appearance of cliques
Non-participation by several members

*These are some of the reasons why, in practice, a meeting should not be too large — certainly not more than ten or twelve — if it is to do its work efficiently. If additional people do have to be brought in — for instance, because their professional advice is needed — they should be involved via sub-committees or through liaison with the chairman.* (An equally effective way of collecting information from people or testing opinion is through questionnaires and surveys.)

**Easy come, easy grow**

Large, unwieldy meetings seem to be especially common in the public sector, perhaps because of legal and representational considerations. A hospital secretary told me about a series of meetings he attended to discuss a new catering block. Participants included (from regional headquarters): *(a)* a medical administrator and his assistant, *(b)* the architect and two assistants, *(c)* three administrators, *(d)* two engineers, *(e)* two nursing officers; and also (from the hospital which was to get the new block): *(f)* five nursing staff, *(g)* four administrators, *(h)* the catering manager and his assistant. A grand total of twenty-three.

Naturally, with this size of membership, progress in meetings was extremely slow; and because the slowness had been anticipated, the meetings had begun many months before the project was due to go on the starts list. Therefore, there was little reliable information available at this early stage, such as how much money was avail-

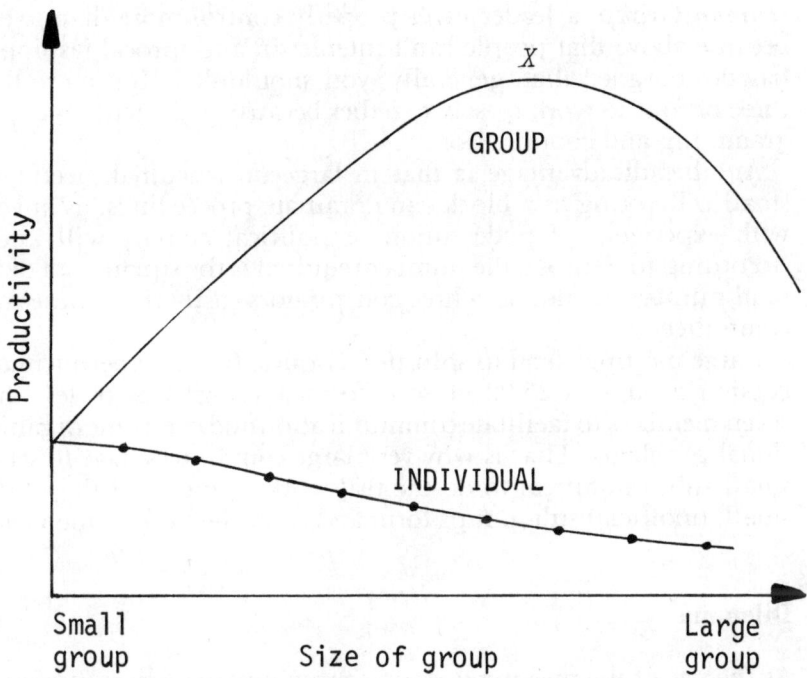

**Figure 16** *At first, as a committee increases in size, efficiency grows. But after a certain size has been passed there are serious 'process' losses, i.e. communication and organisation problems, and productivity, dips. Point X varies with each committee: find it by experimentation.*

able, or the number of people to be catered for. So the same unresolved items appeared on agenda after agenda because the informational tools for dealing with them weren't yet available.

Moreover, with so many people present it was difficult to reach agreement on anything; and even when a decision was taken the facts were likely to change and render it invalid before the next meeting. According to the hospital secretary, the meetings were embarrassingly slow and inefficient because too many people were participating. 'To have made them businesslike', he said, 'their membership would have had to be slashed by sixty or seventy per cent'.

One reason why productivity is usually low in a large meeting is that it needs to spend a lot of time on procedure — otherwise the chairman is likely to lose control. According to Homans in *The*

*Human Group*, a leader can't properly control more than twelve because above that people can't interact in a reciprocal fashion. It has been argued that, generally, you shouldn't assign more than three or four to work closely together because of difficulties of programming and coordination.

Another disadvantage is that in large unstructured meetings a small cell voting as a block can dominate proceedings, as anyone with experience of trade union or political activity will know. According to Penrose, the number required is the square root of the total number attending. Three conspirators easily ride a nine-man committee.

Large meetings tend to split into cliques. In one experiment discussion groups of 15-22 persons formed sub-groups of less than seven members to facilitate communication and overcome organisational problems. That is why very large committees have to set up small sub-committees to do the real work: and even if they don't, small, unofficial sub-groups form and carry the bulk of the work.

## Dilemma

As the size of the meeting goes up the amount of satisfaction felt by members declines because of less participation. Perhaps as a result of this, individual productivity dips. Moede observed members of a group who pulled a rope as hard as possible. At intervals, an extra man was added to the team. With each increase in membership there was a decreased average contribution.

When a group is very small, adding extra members means extra muscle-power: the group works better because of the extra resources. But as more members are added the adrenalin-surge weakens. And beyond a certain point effectiveness decreases as more members are added, because of organisation and communication problems.

*So here is the dilemma that faces the manager of meetings: the meeting has to be big enough to provide the resources needed to do the job; but it has to be small enough to avoid serious organisational and communication problems.*

Trial and error is the quickest and easiest way of discovering the right balance. Over a three month period, say, deliberately vary the size of meetings and estimate which size is best for dealing with particular problems. Remember that there is no 'optimum' size for all purposes and all meetings. There is only an optimum size for inter-

**Table 4**

| Number of participants | Effects on decision-making |
|---|---|
| Two | Biased or freakish decisions are possible. Each person can veto the other's proposals. Fear of alienating the other may lead to pulled punches and too-easy agreement. |
| Three | Pairing can develop three ways and any member is easily outvoted. The odd man out may withdraw into himself and stop being productive, or set up a disruptive protest movement. Meetings of this size lack the error-correcting properties of larger meetings. |
| Four | Sharp cleavages often appear - three against one or two against two. Meetings of this size rarely have enough breadth of experience and thinking to deal adequately with complex problems. A four-man meeting may have great difficulty in reaching a decision because, as games like bridge illustrate, stable competitive groupings of opposed pairs are likely to form. |
| Five to ten | In groups of this size people can talk nearly as much as they want to and exert influence over one another. Free interaction is possible. There is usually sufficient variety of talent and experience to tackle complex problems imaginatively. But a major group may form against a smaller group, and so the problems of minorities are born. |
| Over ten | As the group grows in numbers an increasing number of people are scared into silence. Intimate face-to-face contact between all members becomes impossible, so the meeting tends to split into cliques. Formal procedure is needed to prevent disorder, and this can freeze the interaction and reduce productivity. On the other hand, big meetings can solve certain types of problem better than smaller meetings, e.g. brainstorming, where a large number of ideas are needed initially, or where an averaged estimate is needed. (Gordon found that the larger the group the more accurate its estimate of the weights of objects: individual's errors tend to be cancelled out in accordance with statistical laws.) |

action (small); an optimum size for range and variety of ideas (large); and so on. Thus in achieving the right size of meeting for any particular purpose the first step is to be precise about what that purpose is. The second step is to experiment.

For many purposes, though, meetings of between five and nine members seem to work well. In meetings of this size people can talk nearly as much as they want to and exert influence over each other. Groups of this size waste little time on procedural matters and it is possible to include each person's thinking in the final decision. Yet there is sufficient variety of talent and experience to tackle problems imaginatively. After years of systematic study of the problem, the Laboratory of Social Relations at Harvard reckons that five is the right number for problem-solving meetings. H. Bonner concludes, after a detailed study of the whole question of size, that meetings of between six and ten individuals are the most efficient.

Thomas and Fink, in a review of the literature, found only ten experimental studies that examined the impact of size on quality of decision. Evidence seems to be particularly scarce about large meetings of, say, more than ten [11.2].

Table 4 gives the effects on decision-making of various numbers of participants.

Meetings that are too small or too large are inefficient. Small meetings can usually reach quick agreement, but there is always the chance of freak decisions because the error-correcting properties of larger groups are missing. With their extra resources, large meetings are potentially more productive, but communication and inter-action difficulties can cripple their effectiveness — which is why large committees usually have to form sub-committees to do the real work.

Therefore the meeting needs to be big enough to provide the resources needed to solve the problem but small enough to avoid serious communication difficulties and problems of organisation and control. Experimentation is probably the quickest and easiest way of discovering the most suitable number of members for any particular committee.

But for many purposes, meetings of between five and nine seem to work well: people can talk nearly as much as they want to and influence each other's thinking; and there is usually a wide enough variety of expertise available to deal with a wide range of problems and to solve them imaginatively.

*A good working environment is important because it promotes maximum efficiency. The right size of room, suitable seating arrangements, and even the size and shape of the table can affect the decision-making. For instance, an informal atmosphere is needed for creative problem-solving; and that means a quiet room, comfortable chairs, coffee tables — and coffee.*

# 12
# The working environment

Often a favourable working environment proves to be the errant thread that, when pulled, unravels a committee's skein of success. A good working environment promotes maximum efficiency. But when conditions are bad the meeting may founder.

How many times have you fought off sleep in a cramped, smoky, overheated room and settled for a poor decision just for the sake of getting out quickly? How often have you tried in vain to follow a discussion which is drowned out by the roar of a bulldozer beneath the window? How many times have you called a meeting in a room that you have never used before only to find when the time comes that it is too cold or too small or there are no chairs.

Two or three lonely executives huddling in the corner of a cathedral-sized conference chamber will be as ill at ease and as unproductive as a committee of a dozen people that is required to shoehorn itself into a room resembling a cleaning cupboard. One survey indicates that the size of room preferred by most participants is one that

**Figure 17** *How many times have you fought off sleep in a cramped, smoky, overheated room?*

gives the impression of being comfortably full — not crowded — when everyone is present and sitting round the table.

Because of the regularity with which unsuitable meeting rooms were being used for meetings, one French company has drawn up a list and issued it to all executive staff. It details all the rooms which are available for meetings, where they are, and includes a checklist to show the size of each room and the facilities available in each. More firms should follow this example — or at least help meeting organisers to ensure a favourable working environment by setting aside a number of rooms of varying sizes and situations specifically for meetings.

Another French company which had had many complaints about unsuitable meeting rooms went back to first principles to decide what a meeting room should be like. Boardroom-type tables and sit-up chairs were *out*, comfortable chairs and coffee tables were *in*. Wall-charts, screens and extra electrical sockets were installed. Result: more informality in meetings, fewer communication-blocks, better decisions.

A meeting room needs to be the right size and to have certain basic equipment:

1   Ample electrical sockets for tape recorders, overhead, slide and film projectors, and so on.

**Figure 18**   *The boardroom of Overseas Containers in London and one of the most up-to-date examples of an attempt to produce a working Utopia for top-level decision-makers. The company has tried to provide perfect physical conditions for meetings including sound-proofing, air-condition-ing, controlled lighting and a constant temperature of 70-73°F (using the warmth given off by electric lighting and equipment and by the bodies of the people working in the building)*

2    Paper, pencils, sketch-pads and a wall-chart or black-board. The blackboard should be placed well away from the window so that there is no glare or distraction. A built-in wall screen for films and slides can be a useful extra.
3    Comfortable chairs, though not so comfortable that people settle back and doze off.
4    A number of small tables which can be arranged into any size or shape.

Why not ask committees to experiment with different sizes and shapes of table until they find the sort they most prefer?

## Seating arrangements

When progress in a meeting is slow and there is much side-tracking and private conversation the trouble may stem from the seating arrangements. For instance, the usual arrangement — a rectangular table with the chairman at its head — encourages status-consciousness and this, in turn, inhibits the discussion. In *The Silent Language*, Hall points out that leaders tend to occupy the head position at a meeting with their lieutenants by their side. Opposition or lower-status groups tend to position themselves at the lower end of the table. In joint consultative meetings it is common for the management representatives to sit together at the top end of the table, and the worker representatives to sit at the bottom end of the table opposite them, in confrontation positions. No wonder so many meetings of this kind generate conflict and strain.

A long rectangular table may split a meeting into rival camps, with rival departments or cliques gathered on each side. Not surprisingly, this kind of meeting often turns into a kind of verbal tennis match, with contributions flying to and fro across the table rather than around it. Generally speaking, you talk either to the chairman or to the people opposite, and you respond to comments by the people opposite more than to comments made by people alongside you. So by arranging for rival cliques to be seated on the same side of the table there is less chance of them turning the meeting into a private war-game, simply because they will direct most of their remarks not at their enemies (who are on the same side of the table) but at neutrals (on the other side of the table).

The kind of seating arrangement that allows people to sit directly opposite each other in a meeting can create confrontation and conflict, perhaps because 'direct visual contact represents a challenge to

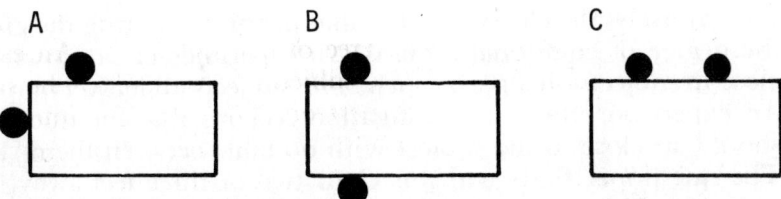

**Figure 19** *The most common seating patterns chosen for A—conversation; B—competitive tasks; C—cooperative tasks. By seating hostile cliques on the same side of the table you can prevent them turning the meeting into their private war-game*

the other, a play at dominance' [12.1]. Hall has observed how a person who merely looks at some other person or group — in a restaurant, say, or on the underground — is often regarded as intruding.

Notice how individuals who are set to work on competing tasks — even an activity as innocuous as a game of chess, say — almost always sit directly opposite one another, as shown in Figure 19.

## How to cool the encounter

When hostile groups clash in committee — an inter-departmental meeting, say, or a management-union meeting — some of the heat can be taken out of the encounter by the simple device of a round-table arrangement. This makes it impossible for the two sides to take up confrontation positions directly opposite each other. And people at a round table tend to feel psychologically closer to each other than when they are sitting facing each other along opposite sides of a rectangle. Thus the round table arrangement encourages compromise and the abandonment of hard-lining.

Those sitting at the corners of squares or rectangles are either squeezed out or find it difficult to become involved in the discussion. A round table arrangement side-steps this danger — or a U-shaped arrangement if the meeting is a large one. The round table can improve the interaction — and so boost the meeting's productivity.

Another way of cooling a heated encounter is to use a very large table, or a number of tables in such a way that the combatants are placed at a distance from one another — as at the Arab-Israeli peace talks in December 1973. You feel foolish pounding the table when the enemy is thirty or forty feet away.

Conversely, the closer together that people are sitting the greater the degree of emotional arousal. An experimenter sat down very close to subjects on a park bench. The subjects all left very rapidly. An expert on criminal investigation reckons that the questioner should sit close to the subject with no table between them [12.2]. The questioner starts with his chair two or three feet away, then moves in closer as the questioning proceeds so that ultimately one of the subject's knees is in between the interrogator's two knees. This invasion causes emotional arousals, putting the suspect into a sweat and destroying his self-confidence.

In very general terms, the most effective seating pattern for a meeting is one that encourages maximum interaction by allowing direct eye contact between all participants — for example, a circular or U-shaped arrangement. The reason why eye contact encourages interaction is that the speaker needs to know whether the listeners understand, believe or disbelieve, are surprised or bored, agree or disagree, are pleased or annoyed. This information is in fact obtained by careful study of the other's face. When the other is invisible these visual signals are unobtainable.


**Trying too hard**

Trying too hard to create the right physical conditions for a meeting can have a boomerang effect. The chairs shouldn't be *too* comfortable or the room *too* quiet. When one company chief found that people were nodding off in meetings he replaced the arm chairs with straight-backs, and secretly had the room temperature lowered by ten degrees. The result, according to him, was sprightlier meetings and better decisions.

An American insurance company decided to create the perfect environment for a meeting, so it arranged for its land-locked executives to attend a management seminar on board a cruise ship. But the meeting had to be abandoned after half an hour because half the executives were prone to sea-sickness.

In the last analysis, the most effective physical conditions for a meeting are any conditions which help the members to make good decisions. Possibly the best place to hold a meeting about where to position new machinery would be on the factory floor. One of the best meetings I ever attended (in terms of results) was a progress meeting to discuss a construction project. The meeting was held in a thin drizzle on top of a mound of rubble and anybody who spoke had to howl to make himself heard above the soothing murmur of the mechanical shovels.

Most meetings, though, are held around a table, and the shape of that table can influence the decision-making. A rectangular table with the chairman at its head encourages status-consciousness, which may silence the lower-status participants, or can turn the meeting into a war game, for different cliques may take up confrontation positions directly opposite each other. With a circular or U-shaped arrangement, confrontation positions are not possible and this encourages compromise. For an informal meeting an informal atmosphere is needed — which means comfortable chairs and coffee tables, or no tables at all.

The meeting room should be the right size, quiet and well equipped. More firms should help to ensure a favourable working environment for their committees by setting aside a number of rooms of varying sizes specifically for meetings.

*Many committees could improve their per-formance by drawing up new and simpler procedural rules. For participants are more likely to be productive when procedure is simple and easy to understand. Too much of it kills creativity and gives influence to the Committee Bore. Procedure makes a positive contribution to a meeting only when it is working like the alchemist's flame, conjur-ing good results out of chaos.*

# 13
# What's the procedure?

Over-heavy procedure can act on a meeting like an anaesthetic. Sometimes it exists as a deadening habit from the past (is that why so many meetings keep minutes and waste hours floundering in the stuff?) and causes influence to fall to those with procedural know how, though they may be empty drums. Inexperienced members get snared in the meshes of the procedural net and become helpless onlookers. The creative person shrinks into his shell, alarmed by the *nem cons* and *ultra vires* and points of order. The Committee Bore flourishes. (One way to take the wind out of *his* cheeks is to impose a time limit on speeches: he uses his time up then shuts up.) Idea-production falls.

These are the effects. Yet the aim of most meetings is to solve problems and make decisions as efficiently as possible; and to make full use of the talents of all members. That is why every committee needs to be more concerned with ideas and people than with conventions and procedures. Ideas are more likely to spark and people are more likely to be productive when procedure is simple and easy to understand.

'An amendment must be proposed in accordance with the following procedure . . .'; 'a point of order arises when . . .'; 'any comments should be strictly relevant to the motion on the agenda sheet' — in the modern world this sort of stuff is as camp as a row of tents. It's ugly and probably useless. Yet some people thrive on it, like collectors drooling over Victoria chamber-pots. 'It is an imperative rule', according to one authority, 'that any amendment must be relevant to the question on which the amendment is proposed.' It must please somebody. But if any committee on which you serve has been snared by its repulsive charms, why not make a bid for freedom — and greater efficiency — by drawing up new and simpler procedural rules?

'Keep strictly to the agenda', goes another traditional rule. Yet often the most rewarding areas of discussion become apparent only as the meeting unfolds: they can't be *predicted* for inclusion on the agenda. In an agenda-bound meeting these fertile areas may remain unexplored.

But constructive not destructive procedure should be the aim: the price is external vigilance and a willingness to ditch convention. Even the House of Lords sees the need for streamlining procedure from time to time. Recently its proceedings have been made simpler and more businesslike. Another welcome innovation has been the prominent placing of two clocks in the chamber as a gentle incentive to their lordships to be short-winded.

Procedures at top government level, too, have been improved in recent years. Cabinet Ministers, for instance, have traditionally gone into Cabinet meetings largely uninstructed on matters that didn't directly concern their own departments. But the machinery for adequately briefing them has now been set up — the Think Tank. How many political disasters in the past sprang from inadequate Cabinet briefing procedure?

Procedure should be made to earn its keep: either it helps committee members with their work or it goes. Why not apply that simple test to the committees on which you serve?

## When procedure helps

No committee ever has a good idea. Ideas are produced by people. Committees can only adopt them. Thus the main objective of a problem-solving meeting should be to create the conditions in which ideas flourish and to make sure that individuals don't feel hemmed in by over-heavy procedure. How often have you stifled your own ideas in meetings for fear of breaking one of the many rules?

But procedure can, when carefully devised, give the problem-solver extra muscle-power. For instance, procedure and structure offer the only hope of dealing adequately with certain complex problems. For they ensure synchronised thinking and systematic coverage. Whereas, if participants were allowed to speak 'freely' in a completely unstructured way, the subject might fragment with each individual pursuing his own pet ideas. Thus any attempt at *analytical* problem solving (see Chapter 5) would be impossible.

Imagine that you are to chair a meeting called to review some important capital expenditure projects. You realise that the only way you can deal adequately with a problem of this size is to analyse its *components* separately: in this way the members will gradually see the problem as a whole as one building block is dropped on top of another.

So you decide to carve the discussion into several stages, with a time-limit on each:

1   Review of all current projects — introduced by Projects Manager. *20 min*
2   Progress reports — Site Managers. *15 min*
3   Estimated costs and expenses — Management Accountant. *10 min*
4   Possible economies — discussion. *45 min*
5   Conclusions and recommendations. *30 min*

Norman Maier has found that this kind of developmental approach to complex problems leads to better decisions than a 'free' unstructured approach. In some meetings, structure, centralised control and restricted communication are necessary for efficiency.

Rules, procedures, set dates and times of meetings and a regular chairman and agenda create stability and clarity — conditions which can help a committee to cope with complex problems within a rapidly changing environment.

Moreover, as a field study of 72 committees in different organisations showed, participants feel a greater sense of satisfaction if meetings are run to a pattern, with set rules of procedure. No doubt one reason is that these ensure that everyone gets a fair hearing.

### Procedure: the alchemist's flame

Procedure is useful when it works like the alchemist's flame, conjuring good results out of chaos. Or when it acts as a lens, enabling people to see a complex problem clearly. The creative use of procedure in a meeting involves using rules to make sure that ideas are encouraged, protected and properly assessed.

A certain amount of structure and formal procedure also allows a meeting to deal speedily and efficiently with a certain kind of agenda — particularly one which consists of a series of easy items. Case for/case against/decision is one way of structuring the discussion on each item.

Bavelas invented a simple game requiring the exchange of information. He noticed that the performance of groups playing the game varied according to the way each group was organised. For instance, when everybody could communicate with everybody else and there was no specific leader, the group took a long time to complete the task. If, by contrast, members of the group communicated only with one person, the leader, they performed the task much more quickly — although the price to be paid for efficient procedure was low morale (except for the man in the centre, who enjoyed himself hugely).

Structure and centralised control can help a meeting to find a speedy solution to certain kinds of problem.

A structured approach is particularly necessary when a committee is working under pressure of time or in a competitive environment. In an advertising agency, meetings of the 'creative' people are usually pretty informal and unstructured — feet-on-the-table style and first-name terms all round. But as soon as two competing teams are asked to produce rival campaigns for approval by an outside client they quickly opt — in my experience at least — for centralised direction and a structured approach to the problem.

Some meetings require very strict procedure, and especially when questions of consent and representation are involved — for instance, at a shareholders' meeting or at an AGM. On these occasions, procedures provide safeguards against malpractices and ensure fair play between opposing interests.

### The case for formal procedure

Often formal procedure can prevent a meeting dissolving in con-

*The feet-on-the-table style of meeting: happy but unproductive*

flict. For instance, when a highly controversial subject is being debated — the kind that touches off intense emotions — or when a meeting splits into two gloweringly hostile camps. Having to observe strict rules, address one's remarks to the chair, and so on, takes much of the heat out of the discussion.

Very large meetings require strict procedure if decisions are to be hammered out of the wide range of opinions and interests represented. Thus Hemphill found that groups with more than thirty members are willing to accept centralised control because they realise that chaos is the likely alternative.

Very large gatherings — political or trade union conventions and the like — couldn't function without carefully contrived procedural rules to suit the occasion. Often they set up a special sub-committee to draw up these rules.

But the procedure used in the House of Commons is the kind most widely used for controlling large meetings. This can be varied to suit the particular needs of the meeting, provided that the two basic principles are observed. These are: (1) the majority opinion is accepted but (2) minority views should be heard.

Very formal procedure is useful for controlling large public meetings. It usually involves:

1    Each item for discussion is introduced by a formal motion.
2    Adequate discussion time is allowed. All points of view are heard. In a controversial, two-sided debate, an alternating pattern of speakers, pro and con, usually works well.
3    The motion is restated.
4    A vote is taken on the motion.

These are some of the reasons why a committee chairman needs a working knowledge of the rules of formal assemblies. Most of the formal procedure used in meetings is based on parliamentary procedure. Erskine May's *Parliamentary Practice* and Palgrave's *Chairman's Handbook* are the authoritative works on the subject.

Perhaps the most serious limitation of formal procedure is that motions put forward to be winnowed by voting are alternatives to one another. Adopting one usually means rejecting the others. But often, in less formal discussions, the best solution combines points from several proposals — the consensus view.

### 'Natural' procedure

In practice, most committees rely on the rule book to some extent. Or, where nobody flourishes the rule book, on *unwritten* procedures as a way of solving communication problems. Thus Bales found that groups develop a kind of natural procedure when solving problems, even in the absence of any imposed rules [13.1]. In tackling the problem they tend to go through an ordered sequence:

1   The assembly of a pool of information about the facts of the case.
2   The formation of common opinions and evaluations of the situation.
3   Finally, after the groundwork has been done, the consideration of specific suggestions.

Perhaps another reason why procedure seems to evolve naturally in a committee is that the members themselves welcome a degree of formality because it means that they don't have to exert themselves to obtain a fair hearing. Formal procedure seems to be especially welcomed by participants during the early stages of a committee's life. At that time, formal procedure has the great advantage of helping a group of people to start working together without delay. It also enables many of the initial communication problems to be by-passed — who speaks and when; how the problem should be approached; etc.

Procedure can make life easier for committee members. For fewer decisions have to be taken (as when sitting at a conveyor belt). People are clear about what they should say and do. Other people's behaviour is more predictable and conflict is suppressed. It makes for cosy meetings, but, when used on the wrong occasion, can inhibit the discussion and lead to poor decisions.

**Degrees of procedure**

One of the essential skills of managing meetings is knowing *how much* procedure each meeting requires — and being willing to impose it in practice. For each problem — and each committee — has a degree of procedure that exactly suits it. That is why the chairman (or the manager who called the meeting), needs to be sensitive to people's preferences.

*Some people prefer a good deal of procedure and a structured, analytical approach. Others prefer more 'wide-open' methods. But remember that as members get to know each other they develop a group approach to problem-solving, and increasingly they prefer* unwritten *procedures that they have created for themselves.*

Not every chairman has enough experience or expertise to range across the whole procedural keyboard at will. This is one of the reasons why many companies invite an experienced outsider to become chairman of the board; and why a lay chairman is sometimes appointed to chair a government scientific or investigating committee. The appointment ensures expert chairmanship, a disinterested approach — and the right sort of procedure for the occasion.

Some people are more productive and active when procedure is simple and easy to understand. Too much procedure may simply hand influence to the Committee Bore, whereas the creative, sensitive person is scared into silence.

A complete absence of procedure implies unrestricted communication. This may create a battleground of ideas, which is good. Or it may simply create a background din that prevents any ideas being heard at all — as when the committee is immature or too large. Mature groups, which have worked through their most serious emotional problems, usually work well together without the need for procedural controls. But immature groups, i.e. groups that are still experiencing serious inter-personal difficulties, need procedure to prevent meetings from being destroyed by tension and conflict or paralysed by inhibition and withdrawal.

A committee should simplify its procedural rules when they are having the effect of slowing down the proceedings or inhibiting the discussion. For procedure should act as a catalyst, creating order — and solutions — out of the chaos. If it fails in this then it becomes a time-wasting ritual, as undesirable as red tape or an obsolete filing system.

**Voting or consensus?**

Perhaps the most important of all procedural questions is how the decisions in meetings are to be made — by consensus or majority vote. Voting is *essential* when questions of consent are involved — the appointment of officers at an AGM, for instance. It is *useful* when it would be difficult to reach a decision by consensus. (Voting resolves crises in much the same way as at a General Election.) Voting is also a quick and easy way of testing how people feel about any particular issue.

But there are many disadvantages and risks in making decisions by majority vote:

1   Different cliques may map out spheres of influence and do secret deals — 'You vote for our man and we'll vote for yours'.
2   Issues are made to seem black or white because members have to be either for or against a proposal. Balance and consensus shades of grey disappear. All or nothing choices are made.
3   Participants may censor their own ideas because they don't want to be on the losing side.
4   A meeting may split into cliques — For and Against. Instead of tackling problems together, opposing sides spend much time and energy trying to outwit each other. Knowing that there is going to be a vote pushes you into taking up a 'position' in advance.
5   As the experience of some trade unions shows, small determined groups may develop tactics for winning votes and decisions, thus manipulating the meeting for their own ends.

When a quick decision is forced by a vote you get a majority and a minority — and a decision, which the defeated minority may unconsciously (or quite consciously) reject. Unconscious rejection often comes at the implementation stage: the defeated groups may manipulate the outcomes to 'prove' just how wrong the decision was.

Consensus agreements can be reached surprisingly often if members agree to settle their differences one point at a time. But where there is an underlying value-gap — as when representatives from different political parties meet, for instance, or when management meet militant unionists — no mere technique is going to make agreement by consensus possible. When, in cases like these, consensus is clearly impossible, why not try to get all the members of the meeting to accept that a decision of one kind or another is called for and that all of them will support the decision once it has been reached by voting?

*Some meetings require only minimal fore-thought and planning whereas others require weeks of painstaking preparation. But an essential first step in planning any meeting is to clarify the objectives in your own mind — and to make sure that the participants are equally clear about them. For people work hard in meetings when they are clear about objectives and feel that they are important. Other key tasks are drawing up the agenda, preparing working papers and drafting the notice of the meeting.*

# 14

# Some preparatory chores

In a Japanese radio factory, managers and specialists attend voluntary unpaid meetings on most weekday evenings. The idea of the meetings is to find ways of improving product designs and cutting costs so that the company stays competitive in overseas markets — despite revaluation of the yen, which has led to prices becoming less competitive. *People willingly attend these meetings because they are convinced of the importance of the objectives.*

One of Field Marshal Montgomery's ironclad rules was that the plan of campaign should be known to every soldier and discussed by all ranks so that everybody would fight with a will.

People spur themselves to greater efforts when they are clear about objectives and feel that they are important. That is why an essential first step in planning your meeting is to clarify the objectives in your own mind, then to make sure that the other participants are equally clear. Thus the following sequence of actions might be required:

1   Well in advance of the meeting, discuss objectives with senior managers and with one or two key members.
2   Briefly state the objectives as agreed in these informal discussions in the memo which gives notice of the meeting.
3   Phone or call on each participant and discuss objectives in more detail.
4   Start the meeting by discussing objectives to make sure that there is a common understanding of what they are.

In clarifying the objectives in your own mind, ask yourself: Is this meeting really necessary? Could I achieve the same results more cheaply or more efficiently by some other method, such as delegation or written communication?

For instance, you consider calling a meeting to explain a new incentive scheme, until you decide that you could do the job more efficiently and cheaply by circulating a memo containing full details of the scheme, and briefing foremen so that they will be able to explain the details to their sections and answer questions.

Exactly what are you hoping to get from the meeting — a decision, a recommendation, an allocation of resources? Knowing the answer may tell you which people to invite, what size the meeting should be, when to hold the meeting, style of chairmanship required, and so on. For instance, a meeting with clients or another department aimed at winning goodwill needs an informal style of chairmanship.

Again, once you are clear about the objectives you should be able to estimate the time-scale required for achieving them — for instance, that a short one-off meeting will be sufficient or, alternatively, that four or five meetings will be required. If a series of meetings is likely, you will need to start thinking about which sub-objectives you want to achieve in each one:

*Overall objective*: To reform divisional structure so that administrative and production bottlenecks are eliminated and staff-cuts of 10-20% are possible. Approximately six meetings required.

*Sub-objectives*:
*First meeting*: Discuss objectives with participants (who include heads of all departments likely to be affected): try to reach shared understanding of what the objectives are and their importance.

*Second meeting*: Analyse problems caused by present structure.

*Third and fourth meetings*: Report by each department head on administrative and production problems and suggested methods of eliminating them.

*Fifth and sixth meetings*: Discussion of possible solutions; formulation of outline proposals for reform.

Careful thinking about objectives is necessary because a meeting brings together a number of individuals. Each has his own personal goals and ambitions and way of looking at things. Unless all are agreed, at an early stage, on a single over-riding purpose, the discussion may well become fragmented as each individual talks about what *he* thinks is important and presses his own ideas and pet theories.

## Planning the meeting

One of the skills of managing meetings is the ability to gauge the amount of preparation that is required. Unplanned meetings can, of course, be very successful. But when they are, it is usually through sheer good luck.

Even meetings called at very short notice require a minimum of strategic and tactical planning for success. A short briefing session may require no more than a few seconds' thought about content and sequence, and one or two notes scribbled on the back of an envelope. At the other end of the scale, a meeting called to plan a forthcoming merger, or an AGM, may take weeks or months of painstaking preparation. Joint meetings between different organisations may require talks about talks — preliminary meetings between representatives from both sides to agree on terms of reference, topics for discussion, who should attend, what information is required by participants and so on.

Plan your meeting in the spirit of the job analyst who assesses a task, decides how it should be tackled and what kind of skills should be allocated to it. Think of the kind of problems the meeting will be dealing with — technical or non-technical, simple or complex, routine or unusual. This may tell you the kind of people who should be invited — from what kind of function and from what levels in the organisation. What kind of skills will be needed to deal with the problems facing the meeting, and can these skills be provided by the organisation? If, for instance, you have called a meeting to discuss a proposal to install closed-circuit television or a centralised dicta-

*Don't invite people to meetings merely because they 'talk well'*

tion facility you may well find that there is nobody inside the organisation who is really competent to assess the alternatives properly, and you may need to invite an outside expert from a manufacturing company or a specialist agency to attend the meeting for the purpose of briefing the members. (Remember that to be an expert, 'you merely have to arrive from outside professing to be one. You are never put to a test which cannot be bluffed out) [14.1].)

The trick is to match the members and the problem; to range widely and make full use of the organisation's human resources when selecting the people who are to attend the meeting and who will be carrying out the decisions taken during the meeting. This requires a thorough knowledge of the organisation and the different skills represented in it.

Hitting on a suitable time and date may require some preliminary phoning and footwork. Take a moment to think about the individuals' workloads, their schedules and their preferences; ring their secretaries to find out which days are most likely to be free; and *then* fix a date and time for the meeting.

Inviting people to attend because of their status or on the basis of a loud voice and confident manner is inefficient management. One manager I used to know approached the selection problem by packing all his meetings with the most senior people who happened to be free at the time, under the mistaken impression that this would ensure a high-powered meeting. But the usual result was a room packed with senior executives, staring in puzzlement at the chairman and wondering why so many problems were being lofted to them from the operating level: an example of poor planning leading to a bored meeting (and incidentally, mediocre decisions).

Table 5 tabulates the foregoing points.

**Table 5**

| Level of meeting | Type of decision | Who to invite |
|---|---|---|
| Top level | 1 General policy decisions<br>2 Long-term strategic decisions, e.g. where to site a new plant<br>3 Decisions affecting the whole organisation | Directors; senior executives; general managers |
| Middle level | 1 Medium-term managerial decisions, e.g. purchase of equipment<br>2 Decisions affecting a part of the organisation or a particular function | Department heads; middle managers; technical specialists |
| Junior level | 1 Operating decisions, e.g. eliminating a production bottleneck<br>2 Day-to-day administrative decision | Junior managers and administrators; foremen and supervisors; technical specialists |

### Check the meeting's powers

One essential preparatory step is to check the meeting's authority:

Can the meeting take decisions? Or is it only empowered to make recommendations to some higher body?

What kind of decisions can it take? Routine decisions? Decisions involving small-scale expenditure? Or major decisions such as authorising new work programmes, allocating men and money to new projects, and so on?

Are there any financial or political constraints on the decision-making, such as budgets which must not be exceeded; or a hostile manager who will have to be squared before a particular decision is taken?

Have the participants — individually or collectively — got enough leverage in the organisation to ensure that decisions will get translated into action, e.g. that staff and funds will be forthcoming to carry out the decision. If not, better take another look at your invitation list.

### The agenda

Without an agenda, the meeting may lack direction and purpose. People will tend to contribute in a haphazard way — talk about what interests them personally rather than analysing a problem systematically or working through a programme. Such a pattern is disastrous when the aim of the meeting is not just to talk around a problem but actually to solve it.

An agenda gives structure to the proceedings, breaks the discussion into a number of logical and manageable stages, moves the meeting gradually towards a solution or through a programme. Even a meeting called to discuss a single subject can gain points and coherence with an agenda to ensure a balanced appraisal of the problem.

When drawing up the agenda, be realistic about the number of items that can be covered in the time available.* Don't make the mis-

* Usually the committee secretary — if there is one — draws up the agenda in consultation with the chairman.

take of thinking that you can add efficiency by cramming extra items onto the agenda sheet. Such a meeting looks good on paper but in practice leads to over-hasty decision making. Meetings need time to deal with complex problems: under pressure, they settle for quick but unsound decisions. The National Industrial Conference Board discovered that many meetings fail simply because the chairman keeps them going too fast and fails to give the group time to develop its own solution.

If a long list of topics must be discussed why not hold a number of short separate meetings: each one would have its own precise objective and selected membership — and a short manageable agenda.

My own system for estimating the time required for working through a particular agenda is

1    Estimate the time required to deal with each item.
2    Calculate the total time required.
3    Double this figure.

To ensure that the meeting finishes promptly and that the whole agenda will be covered in the time available, why not set a time limit for discussion of each item? (Even then it pays to be flexible, to be prepared to break the schedule if necessary: with certain topics, for instance, the most rewarding areas of the discussion can never be anticipated and allowed for: when they crop up extra time may need to be given to them.)

Don't shorten the agenda simply by leaving pressing items off it. For people will probably raise them in any case, either under Any Other Business or earlier, which can disrupt the meeting.

Try to make sure that all the items on the agenda concern the entire membership. Any topics that concern only a few of the participants could probably be dealt with more efficiently in a smaller, separate meeting.

Place routine items at the top of the agenda sheet: they will be quickly dealt with, leaving the rest of the time available for discussion of the two or three important items. Or a certain order may be needed so that busy people, who will be contributing to only two or three items, will be able to come along at the appropriate time, then leave when there is no further need to remain.

Once the agenda has been drawn up, send it to members two or three days before the meeting, so that they have time to brief themselves on the topics, lobby, test opinion and so forth.

Do you need to brief *yourself* on any items on the agenda sheet so that you can answer questions and control the discussion in an intelligent way?

## Working papers

One department head has a strict rule for staff meetings: no topic can be discussed unless essential background information has already been circulated. This manager argues that unless the basic facts are known any discussion becomes a mere pooling of ignorance.

It has been said that there are three sides to every question — the pro side, the con side and the inside. Make sure that your working papers (documents pre-circulated to members and containing essential background information) tell the inside story. This means that the chairman must have access to the company's vital statistics and data and it explains why a committee can only work efficiently and make sound decisions if it has the full support of top management, i.e. they are prepared to make full information available and to accept its recommendations. *Keeping on good terms with senior managers in the company is one of the most important of the committee chairman's jobs.*

High-quality information leads to high-quality decisions. Thus the writing of working papers is a vital preparatory chore. Perhaps the easiest and quickest way of doing this job is to ask the person presenting a particular proposal to provide you with the essential background facts. It then becomes your job to transform this basic raw material into a short, punchy document that gives the plain facts of the case — which picks out the vital data, the main alternatives, the basic arguments. If you lack sufficient time to do this editing job properly why not delegate it to one of your staff or to some other member of the committee?

Some notes in tabular form giving hints on how to prepare working papers are given in Table 6. During the preparation the members' information needs and the level of their education should be borne in mind. If writing for technical experts, you can be free with technical terms and assume that they grasp the basic assumptions. If you are writing for laymen, however, you should take nothing for granted and lay the foundations carefully.

Working papers should be attached to the memo giving notice of the meeting. The memo is an important document because so often it is the only source of information about the meeting that members have. Design it so that it gives the basic facts about the meeting as clearly and succinctly as possible. Make sure that it gives the following information:

Time, place and date.

Table 6

| PREPARING WORKING PAPERS | |
| --- | --- |
| For top-level meetings | For lower-level meetings |
| 1 Investigate the financial aspects thoroughly. Carefully research costs, prices, depreciation, credit terms, effects on profits, etc. | 1 Investigate the technical or administrative aspects thoroughly, e.g. the precise specifications, the precise procedural changes, etc. |
| 2 Make the information general, e.g. the effect of a particular policy on production over a twelve-month period. Details can be added by means of an oral report to the chairman or or by sending the appropriate expert or official to the meeting to answer questions. | 2 Make the information particular. Give as many concrete details as possible, e.g. a breakdown of maintenance costs, section by section. Keep saying, 'For example...', then add the detail. |
| 3 Present the working paper in such a way that it can be used as a top-level decision-making tool, e.g. give several broad alternative courses of action, together with the major implications of adopting each one (effects on turnover, sales, etc.). | 3 Present the working paper so that its relevance to a particular part of the organisation and to particular managers is clear, e.g. show how the decision will affect the staffing situation in the section, the precise changes of responsibility involved, etc. |

From: A. Barstow, Sales Director  Date: 4 May 1975
  To: G.R.Armitage
      F.Cartwright
      B.J.Moran
      T.E.Phillips
      K.K.Stedman
Copies to: Production Manager
           Unit Heads

Subject: Sales trip to Eastern Europe

1.  Please will you attend a meeting in Room 216 at
    2.45 pm on 7 May 1975.
2.  The purpose of the meeting is to discuss our
    strategy during our forthcoming trip, and in
    particular (a) the terms we should offer to our
    Polish customers, (b) how we should reply to the
    Rumanian request and (c) credit arrangements.
3.  The meeting will probably last most of the
    afternoon.

                              A. Barstow

**Figure 20**  *Memo format*

        Probable duration of the meeting.
        Topics for discussion.
        Purpose of the meeting.
        Name of participants.
   An example of such a memo is shown in Figure 20. Send the
memo to members, together with the agenda and any working papers, three or four days before the meeting.

**Other chores**

The remaining preparatory chores are straightforward enough.
Check that the room you want will be available (the right size of
room is one which gives the impression of being comfortably full
when all the participants are present). Make sure that the lighting is

adequate and that the room is equipped with adequate electrical sockets, has a blackboard, wall-chart, overhead slide or film projector, or any other items that you will require: otherwise arrange for these to be brought in specifically for the meeting. If you plan to use a projector, give as much notice as possible to the operator. Check that tea ladies, caretakers and other ancillary staff whose help you need will be available.

Should you supply pads, pencils, ash trays, water jugs and glasses? Should you arrange for tea or coffee to be served — a big incentive to stay alert in a long meeting.

Make a deliberate decision about seating arrangement — perhaps a round-table or U-shaped arrangement for a creative problem-solving session; theatre-style for a large briefing session, etc. Make another deliberate choice about any special procedure required, e.g. time limit on discussion, vote or consensus, etc., and about the style of chairmanship to be used, e.g. democratic or authoritarian.

Well in advance of the meeting consult those managers who are likely to be affected by any of its decisions. Listen to their opinions and suggestions and consider incorporating these into the proposals, thus reducing the chance of sabotage at the implementation stage.

*Regular coffee breaks prevent 'fading' — even in a long meeting*

**Control aids**

Could you add interest to the meeting and make it easier to control by arranging for any of the following visual aids to be available?

*A blackboard:* an invaluable aid for controlling the discussion because as soon as a good idea emerges you can 'fix' it on the blackboard before it is swept away in the flow of discussion. Members will be able to focus on it and develop it. The blackboard is useful for listing constraints on the decision-making and for reminding members of the progress they are making.

*A felt or vinyl board* has the same uses as a blackboard. But while letters and illustrations take some time to arrange (they are attached by an adhesive) they give a more polished effect, so that this kind of board is more suitable for an important presentation to a client, say, or for a large, formal meeting such as a sales conference.

*An easel pad:* large sheets of newsprint mounted on an easel allow drawings and diagrams to be carefully prepared well before the meeting. Once a chart has been used in the meeting it can be flipped over for later use or simply ripped off and thrown away.

*Flip-chart:* hinged squares of stiff white paper which can be stood on the table top and flipped at the appropriate moment to reveal a prepared drawing or diagram. The effect is a kind of running visual commentary on the proposal.

*Slides* are useful in very large meetings when charts would be too small. They can be made cheaply and quickly simply by photographing a drawing, diagram or typed sheet of paper.

**The pre-meeting chores: a checklist**

1  Am I clear about the objectives of the meeting? Are the other participants clear about them?
2  Am I clear about the power of the meeting. Has it got authority to take decisions? If so, what kind of decisions? Are there any political or financial constraints on the decision-making?
3  Which people, other than the participants, need to be consulted or informed about the meeting, e.g. other managers who

may be affected by the decisions outside experts, technicians and caretakers?

4 Which items should be included on the agenda? Should they be in any particular order. Should there be a curfew on the discussion of any items?

5 How thoroughly should I brief myself on each item so that I can chair the meeting in an intelligent way. How thoroughly should members be briefed on each item?

6 Whose help do I need in preparing *(a)* working papers, *(b)* the agenda?

7 Which is the most convenient time for the participants to attend?

8 Should a record of the meeting be kept. If so, what kind of record, e.g. minutes recording decisions or short report outlining the main arguments? Should I brief someone to do this chore?

9 Is a particular procedure required? Is a particular style of chairmanship required, e.g. democratic or authoritarian?

10 Is confidentiality required? If so, how can I ensure this?

11 Which files letters or other documents should I take into the meeting in case of awkward questions?

12 Have I invited people to attend the meeting because of the skills and experience they can contribute, rather than because of status or a confident manner?

*By varying his style of chairmanship to meet the needs of the moment the chairman becomes a man for all meetings. When a new committee first meets, an authoritarian style is needed to reduce uncertainty and overcome the communication problems that beset any group of people working together for the first time. But democratic chairmanship is needed during creative problem-solving, when an informal atmosphere is required. Thus the key to competent chairmanship is flexibility. Like the dominant child in Merei's play groups, the chairman needs to subject himself to the needs and preferences of others. The price of control is submission.*

# 15
# Styles of chairmanship

Eugenio Cefio is President of Italy's largest industrial corporation, and such a shy and retiring man that he is known to his employees as 'the ghost'. He is so unassertive that he signs 'The President' on company documents rather than his own name. He leaves all news conferences, speech-making and other ceremonies to his subordinates because, he says sourly, 'It's the middle-ranking people who want to be the prima donnas'.

Another top executive who prefers to exercise control from backstage is Pierre Liotard-Vogt who controls a food empire — Nestle's — second only to that of Unilever. Yet, like thousands of other outstanding executives, this extremely quiet and self-effacing man simply doesn't measure up to the common or Hollywood concept of leadership. This portrays a thrusting dynamism and shimmering iridescence that observation rarely justifies.

In the committee room just as in the boardroom, the all-purpose leader has escaped detection. In the committee room, indeed, there is no clear separation of leader and led. Imagine six men in a meeting. One explains an idea and the others listen. The man with the idea becomes the momentary leader. Then somebody else speaks, develops the point or outlines an alternative method, and leadership passes to him. Thus leadership in the meeting is as momentary and shifting as the flow of discussion itself.

But making sure that the discussion as a whole moves in the required direction demands another kind of leadership — from the chairman. The second kind of leadership implies the ability to plan and control the entire meeting; and, paradoxically, this kind of control may require the gentle touch, even self-effacement.

### Who leads whom?

The dominant child in Merei's play-groups acquired authority by subjecting himself to the will of the others [15.1]. He gained control of the group at the cost of submission. Who led whom?

The chairman of a meeting needs to be equally sensitive to the needs and preferences of his members; to be willing and able to vary his leadership style according to the needs of the moment. This means constantly testing the pulse of the meeting then intervening as required — as rule-maker, conciliator, coordinator, or whatever.

Effective control begins when, at the beginning of the meeting, the chairman sizes up the situation, decides what kind of leadership is required, then slips into the appropriate gear. So in one meeting he is an unassertive idea-eunuch: in the next, a tough, fast-talking overlord. Today he is a suction-pump drawing out people's ideas. Tomorrow he is a conveyor-belt, feeding the group with information, carrying them steadily and efficiently towards a decision. The day after he becomes a spark-plug, showering the meeting with ideas. By discreet use of the loud and soft pedals he becomes a man for all meetings.

Imagine that you have three meetings booked for next week. They have different objectives so will require different approaches:

*First meeting:* a briefing session. You have the facts, they don't, so you do the most of the talking and limit staff participation to a question-and-answer session at the end. Style required: authoritarian.

*Second meeting:* a problem-solving meeting to consider ways of boosting sales. You provide the members with broad alternatives but leave them to make the final choice: they will have to implement any decisions so they had better be decisions they support. You keep the meeting small to encourage maximum interaction, and establish an informal atmosphere so that the ideas will flow freely. You impose only as much structure as is needed to ensure that all the alternatives are properly considered. Style required: democratic.

*Third meeting:* a gripe-session with some of your staff who complain about bonus and overtime arrangements. Your objective is to give them the chance to express their feelings. You recognise that any decision taken at this meeting will be less important than the emotional release it provides. So you adopt a laissez-faire style, refrain from controlling the discussion at all, let the men speak spontaneously.

When three such topics occur on the agenda of the same meeting, the trick is to change your style as you move from one topic to the other.

## Reasons for meeting

Basically there are only five or six reasons for holding meetings: to give or exchange information; to solve problems; to make decisions; to express feelings or opinions; to negotiate.

1  *Giving or exchanging information.* The meeting needs to be highly structured, with the chairman remaining at the centre of the discussion and controlling the participation. You know exactly what ground has to be covered, and a fair degree of autocratic control is necessary to ensure that the talk doesn't become chat, and that the proceedings don't stretch over into a social occasion. An autocrat is needed to sweep irrelevancies aside and to keep the information flowing.

2  *Problem-solving.* The amount of structure that you impose varies with the kind of problem. Generally, 'unstructured' problems that have no correct answer ('How can we generate new business?') require unstructured proceedings and democratic chairmanship (see Chapter 5).

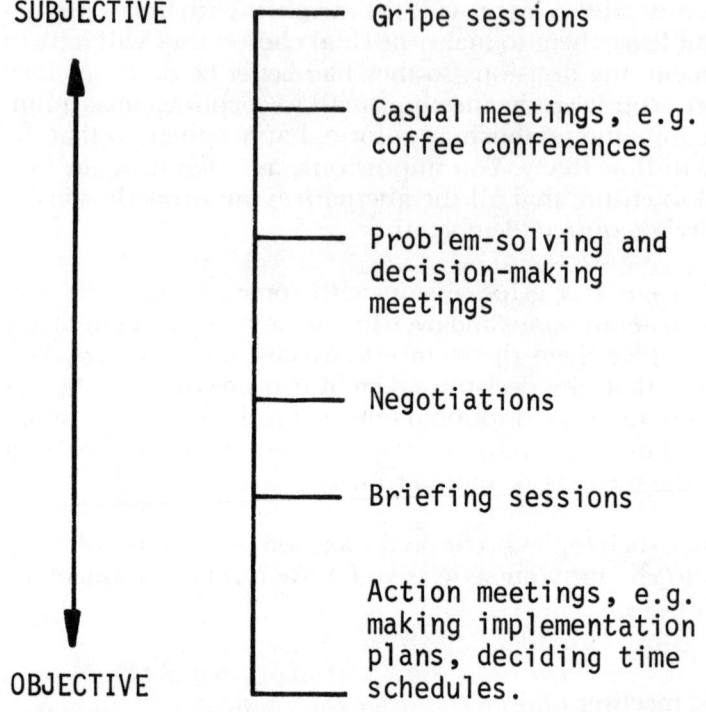

**SUBJECTIVE**

— Gripe sessions

— Casual meetings, e.g. coffee conferences

— Problem-solving and decision-making meetings

— Negotiations

— Briefing sessions

— Action meetings, e.g. making implementation plans, deciding time schedules.

**OBJECTIVE**

**Figure 21** *'Subjective' meetings are held to satisfy the needs of the participants so require little or no structure or control. 'Objective' meetings are held with a specific goal in mind and need as much structure and control as are needed to achieve it*

3 *Decision-making.* The chairman may need to carve the discussion into distinct stages to ensure that all relevant aspects are covered and all the alternatives properly assessed. He may need to control participation to ensure that everyone contributes and that contributions occur in a logical sequence. The main aim is to arrive at a high-quality decision.

4 *Gripe-session.* The chairman tries to establish a *laissez-faire* atmosphere, i.e. permissive and unstructured. He remains in the background and allows members to contribute spontaneously, for he recognises that any decision taken is less important than *(a)* providing a therapeutic opportunity for staff to express their feelings *(b)* ensuring that any decisions taken are acceptable to the participants.

5    *Negotiation.* Without structure and tight control, tempers
could flare and the meeting could get out of control. Structure
is needed so that each side's case is heard in full and without
interruption, and so that the points at issue are isolated, then
discussed singly and in a logical sequence. So you might divide
the discussion into these stages:

a    Side A states its case in full and without interruption.

b    Side B asks questions.

c    Side B states its case in full and without interruption.

d    Side A asks questions.

e    Chairman lists points at issue: invites discussion on the
first of these points.

Thus the chairman's role is that of rule-maker and conciliator,
soothing ruffled feelings and suggesting compromises.


**Autocratic style**

Most new committees initially need strong centralised control. By
imposing control and deciding what topics should be discussed, in
which order, how the decision should be made, etc., an autocratic
chairman helps the committee to overcome uncertainty, and the
communication and organisation problems that beset any group of
people working together for the first time. Generally an autocratic
style of chairmanship is most effective:

1    *When a high degree of initiating structure is required* — for
example, to enable a group of strangers to begin working
together without delay. In a new group members are usually
shy and at a loss for words, don't know what to say or how to
begin or what to do — until somebody tells them.

2    *When the meeting is dealing with a series of easy or routine
items.* According to Guetzkow, programmed, repetitive tasks
can be efficiently disposed of in meetings which have much
'structure' and are run by authoritarian methods.

3    *When the meeting is grappling with a complex technical problem:* usually a certain approach is known to yield good solutions, so this is the approach that has to be imposed (for
example, dividing the discussion into certain stages, or split-

*Some chairmen are dictatorial by temperament*

ting the members into sub-groups and asking each to study a particular aspect).

4    *At times of crisis when decisions need to be made in a hurry.* Strong control and structure ensure that the various aspects are dealt with systematically and in the time available.

5    *In very large meetings where much procedure and strong control are needed* if clear decisions are to be hammered out of the wide range of opinions and interests represented.

An authoritarian style is right when it is *assumed* for purposes of control, like the poker player's deadpan; but offensive when it comes naturally and is used on all occasions. For the dictator-by-temperament has ideas on most subjects, and tends to impose them on the meeting by stifling nonconformity and giving extra weight to opinions that match his own. One manager told me:

I served on the projects committee which was chaired by the managing director. He decided what went on the agenda, yet he

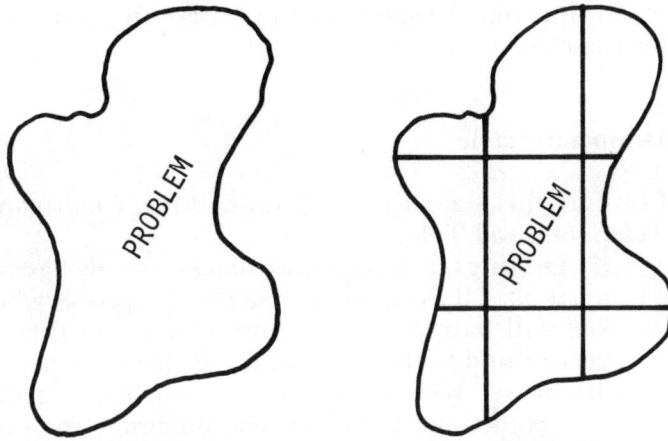

**Figure 22** *Even the simplest structure can secure syste-matic coverage of a problem by requiring that the meet-ing deal with one aspect at a time. This kind of structure is especially important when a meeting is working under time-pressure*

often ignored these items if something else had cropped up in the meantime which he thought was important. So people stopped briefing themselves for meetings. He decided the dura-tion of meetings, yet he often exceeded this if he wanted to carry on talking. He had an overbearing manner and monopolised the meetings. These consisted of a string of his opinions punc-tuated by occasional questions from the other participants.

The National Industrial Conference Board found that the most common pitfalls in meetings are caused by chairman-dominance, and especially when *(a)* the chairman talks too much himself, *(b)* the chairman inhibits free discussion by leading questions and offer-ing suggestions, *(c)* the chairman keeps the meeting going too fast and fails to give the group enough time to develop its own solution.

Another disadvantage of the autocratic style is that it produces submissive behaviour. One marketing director complained: 'When-ever I call a meeting they listen to me too hard. I'll be just speculat-ing that a red can might increase shelf visibility when suddenly the cans *are* red.' Nobody dared to tell this martinet that it was his spe-cial brand of iron-heel chairmanship which was transforming spec-ulation into martial law — and which turned those cans red.

An authoritarian chairman makes quick decisions possible. But much time may be spent later in explaining and winning support for these decisions.

## Democratic style

Consider this statement by John deButts, Chairman of American Telephone and Telegraph:

> (In meetings) I try to be sure that everybody has an opportunity to speak. I'll ask questions so that the people who haven't spoken will have an opportunity to say something . . . . When it gets around to the point where we have reached a consensus, I might say, 'Well, let me try to sum up and see if this is where we are'. Sometimes somebody doesn't agree, and then we have to talk a bit longer. Then I'll try to sum it up again. But a successful meeting depends on how much everybody participates, not on how long it goes on. [15.2].

deButts favours the democratic style because he wants to get all those expensive heads talking. Notice, in particular, the emphasis placed by deButts on reaching decisions by consensus — a major feature of the democratic style.

Many of the most experienced chairmen favour the democratic style for similar reasons. Richard Nixon has described his style of presiding at the Security Council when he was Vice-President:

> I was careful not to express my opinion on any decisions or to cut off the discussions until all the officials present, understandably sensitive about their prerogatives, had their say. Only at the end of the discussion of each subject did I express my own point of view and set forth what I thought was the sense of the meeting as to the decisions which should be made. [15.3]

A democratic style implies minimal structure and control; it means that the chairman is alert to cues from the committee members about what topics should be discussed, in what order, how long the discussion of each one should last, and so on; it means listening, encouraging, being permissive and making little attempt to control the participation. A democratic style of chairmanship is helpful

1  *When political, legal or representational reasons make decision-by-consensus necessary.*
2  *When an informal atmosphere is needed in the meeting* — for instance, in the interests of creative problem-solving.
3  *When the quality of the decision is less important than its acceptability* — e.g. in a meeting called to settle a dispute.

Choice of meeting place, e.g. his own office, with the symbols of his authority openly displayed

**Figure 23** **The authority effect** — *sometimes participants are inhibited by the chairman's manner which — perhaps subconsciously — suggests superior status and authority*

Erect posture, raised head

Haughty facial expression

Staring at people he is speaking to and using a commanding tone of voice

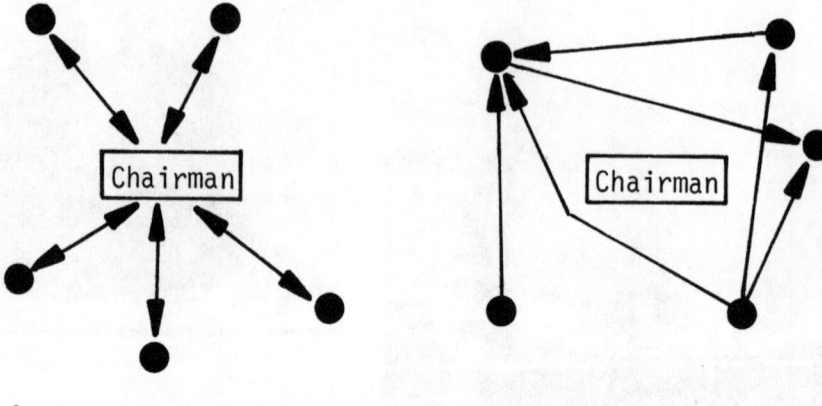

Autocratic style                    Democratic style

**Figure 24**   *Autocratic chairmen stay at the centre of the discussion while democratic chairmen allow free communication. With free interaction the task takes a relatively long time to complete. When the interaction is controlled and members communicate mainly with the chairman, the committee generally performs its task quickly — but often the price to be paid is low morale among the members*

How democratic is your own style of chairmanship? Think back to the last meeting that you chaired. Did you have the impression that people were free to speak their minds? Was there a relaxed and uninhibited atmosphere? Did members continuously defer to their seniors and to the chair? Did you really value the contribution made by each member — and show it? (Effective psychotherapists are warm, permissive, interested in their patients as persons, able to treat them on equal terms as co-workers on common problems [15.4].)

There are times, even in structured meetings, when members want the freedom to kick ideas around spontaneously. Thus in many meetings the best results are obtained by alternating between structured, disciplined progress and relaxed free-wheeling discussion. For instance, a relaxed democratic style may be needed while the meeting is thinking of a solution. But once the meeting has reached the stage of planning the implementation details, it may be ready for structured, controlled participation.

**Techniques to counter dependency**

Sometimes in meetings that require a democratic style of chairman-

AUTOCRATIC ┌ The meeting organiser makes the decision
             and uses the meeting to rubber-stamp it

           ├ The chairman takes the decision on his own
             initiative (although theoretically acting
             on behalf of the committee). This often
             happens in local government

           ├ The committee makes the decision and then
             announces it to the organisation

           ├ The committee makes the decision, but gives
             full reasons and tries to sell it to all
             those affected by it

           ├ The committee first consults people and
             departments who would be affected before
             taking the final decision

             The committee arranges for those most
             likely to be affected to attend meetings
DEMOCRATIC └ and share in the decision-making

**Figure 25**  *The greater the impact of the decision, i.e. the more people who will be affected by it, the more important it is to use a democratic method, thus helping to ensure smooth implementation*

ship to get good results, there are temperamentally submissive people who try to push the chairman into an autocratic role so that, like children, they can enjoy the security of a dependent relationship. (The insecure man loves to fall back into the safe role of follower.) When this happens the chairman may fall into the trap, start to provide all the ideas and make all the decisions — an expensive form of one-man decision-making. But in the interests of productivity, you should refuse to accept total responsibility for the meeting — for instance, by reflecting all requests for ideas and decisions back into the meeting itself:

*Member:* How many more meetings shall we be holding?
*Chairman:* How many more meetings do you think we'll need?
*Member:* Do you think the idea would work out in practice, Mr Chairman?
*Chairman:* I agree — that's the crunch question. What's the answer?

*Another useful technique for countering dependency is to state your own ideas only after all other ideas have been explored so that the members are not constantly trying either to please or to counter the chairman.* For if you talk too early in the meeting the discussion may become a series of reactions to your ideas, pro and con. And even when you do eventually give your own opinions it may be necessary to express them speculatively or to put them in the form of questions:

1   I wonder if we have sufficient resources to undertake a scheme of this size? What do you think?
2   You're recommending a 40 per cent increase in expenditure: is the board likely to agree to that?
3   Do you think a change of policy at this stage would be accept-able to R & D? Who's got an opinion on that one?

The onus is placed on the members to confirm or deny — to reach a conclusion *themselves*.

A recurring symptom of dependency is the opening silence. You open the meeting, outline the problem — then wait for the discussion to begin. But nothing happens. Everybody sits round the table mutely, looking depressed. The embarrassment builds up. Somebody glances at his watch . . . . .

As every chairman knows, the temptation is to plunge nervously into this opening silence and to start analysing the problem, giving information, offering solutions. Unconsciously, you have accepted total responsibility for the success of the meeting, and you find yourself controlling it in a way you never intended, i.e. you *lose* control by appearing to increase it.

The antidote is to refuse to accept responsibility for getting the meeting moving. Throw this responsibility back onto the members themselves. Simply sit in silence with them until somebody speaks. It's wearing on the nerves. But members should emerge from the ordeal with a new sense of responsibility and independence that will improve the problem-solving in future meetings.

Another reason for not intervening is that silence can be positive and creative. After minutes of complete silence there may be a sudden flash, a new cross-fertilising of ideas and the hidden factor is revealed.

Extremely useful for discouraging passive behaviour is the technique of chair rotation. Each member takes his turn to be chairman, and so learns how to lead. But he also learns — by direct experience — about the problems faced by the chairman and, in particular, how the chairman needs the active cooperation and support of the other participants. The insight should spur on temperamentally passive members to be more active and cooperative in their approach during future meetings.

Another way of overcoming passivity is to give each member a particular responsibility or a particular aspect of the problem to report on, so that each man is forced to play a positive and active role. Thomas(1957) found that by creating a division of labour in which members perform complementary roles, a cooperative relation is established between them. This encourages maximum participation by each man and maximum communication between all the members.

Once I served on a committee of seven. One of the members spoke, on average, about once every three meetings. But asking this man to do a feasibility study on a building proposal seemed to release his pent-up energies. He produced a first-rate report describing all the problems and suggesting ways of overcoming them. And he took a major part in the subsequent discussions.

When the quiet type stays in his shell in spite of these methods, he may simply be intimidated by his louder, brasher colleagues, and you may need to discourage and quieten them so as to create more speaking room for him.

## Flexibility is the key

Group influence goes to the man who best fits the occasion. At normal times this may be the steady man. During an unofficial strike the awkward aggressive individual may emerge as leader.

In Bion's study of groups of neurotics during the war often it was the man with the most problems who was the leader. Insane or neurotic politicians are catapulted into leadership in convulsive periods of history. A small, rapidly expanding firm and the giant steady-state corporation require different kinds of chairman. So do different kinds of meeting. For leadership is not a set of permanent qualities enabling one man to march others smartly through the business jungle, for the born leader in one situation — or one meeting — may be reduced to stumbling ineffectuality in another. Josephine Klein sees leadership as the ability to elicit the desired response — and this may require the gentle touch and the leaving of speech-making to others.

The key to competent chairmanship is flexibility. Like the dominant child in Merei's playgroups, the chairman of a meeting needs to subject himself to the needs and preferences of others. He needs to vary his style according to the purpose of the meeting and the preferences of its members. Even in a single meeting the chairman may have to change style as one topic succeeds another.

Generally, an autocratic style is right for meetings dealing with a series of easy items; for tackling complex technical problems; and during the first meetings of a new committee, for it gets a group of strangers working together without delay. A democratic style is more suitable for creative problem-solving; when the acceptability of decisions by participants is the main objective; and when consensus decisions are required (for example, for political reasons, or in the interests of trouble-free implementation).

But as the National Industrial Conference Board found, efficiency can suffer when an autocratic style is used indiscriminately — and especially when the chairman exercises too much control by giving too many opinions and asking too many leading questions.

When submissive participants try to push the chairman into an inappropriately autocratic role, the antidote is to reflect all requests back into the meeting itself; to state one's own ideas only after all other ideas have been explored and, even then, to state them speculatively or in the form of questions. These techniques, like chair rotation and giving specific responsibilities to each member, encourage more active and cooperative participation.

It is also important to sit out the opening silence at the beginning of a meeting, thus thrusting the responsibility for getting the meeting moving onto the members themselves.

It is important to master these techniques for countering submissive behaviour, because without their help the chairman may find himself dominating the meeting in a way that he never intended. This can happen because he exercises such a strong control over the other participants *(a)* by his status as chairman — the authority figure in the meeting, *(b)* by framing and defining the problem initially and *(c)* by controlling participation. Even if he doesn't speak, some members will try to interpret his silences. That is why effective control (and good results) may depend on the chairman's willingness and ability to dilute his own influence.

The Tao-Te-King scripture from China of the sixth century BC states:

> The best soldier is not soldierly
> The best fighter is not ferocious
> The best conqueror does not take part in war
> The best employer of men keeps himself below them

This is called the virtue of not contending
This is called the ability of using men
The best chairman is not always conspicuously in control.

*Sometimes in a meeting the discussion goes round and round. No progress is made. Members talk at cross purposes. Conflict flares up. At times like this the chairman can restore order and a sense of direction provided that he knows — and applies — the control techniques described below. How to resolve conflict, how to stimulate discussion during slack periods, how to squeeze extra work out of members, and the essential technique of time control — these are some of the skills that every chairman must master.*

# 16
# Control techniques

Negative, critical and aggressive remarks occur in every meeting. One expert, for instance, reckons that they account for about 11 per cent of all contributions [16.1]. They are a 'natural' part of group process, providing emotional release, and forcing members to move towards a decision point:

> After a certain point members begin to discourage any new ideas, and subsequently demand general acceptance of the solution. This involves . . . more negative discouraging remarks. [16.2]

Negative remarks can play a *positive* role in meetings. And even if, from the chair, you try to suppress them by ruling them out of order, the ruling will be seen as high-handed or arbitrary and trigger off resentful (negative) reactions. And so the balance is restored.

Criticism may be a natural process in a meeting but it can damage the participants — and the proceedings — simply because people interpret criticism as attack and tend either to withdraw into themselves or to set up a destructive counter-attack. This excerpt from a meeting that I taped shows this response taking place:

> *Member:* You want to see a merger — *(interrupted)*
> *Proposer:* Wait a minute — *(interrupted)*
> *Another member:* You're suggesting a merger of the two departments.
> *Proposer:* In effect, I suppose I am.
> *Member:* It wouldn't work.
> *Another member:* I don't think we can even consider — *(interrupted)*
> *Proposer:* Why wouldn't it work? Have you been doing a feasibility study?
> *(The proposer interprets criticism of the proposal as a personal attack and responds with a sarcastic counter-attack.)*
> *Member:* It wouldn't work because there's no support for the idea in either of the departments.

At this point the skill required by the chairman is the ability to walk on eggs without breaking them — to ensure that the point made about lack of support is properly examined, but without exacerbating the proposer's ruffled feelings. So the chairman might have said something like this (in fact he didn't):

> *Chairman:* I think we should examine the point made about lack of support in a few moments, because it's obviously an important one. But before we start talking about possible snags, I wonder if we could think about the advantages of merging the two departments. Perhaps the proposer could describe the advantages as he sees them.

The chairman discourages premature criticism by earmarking the support issue for later attention. And he creates speaking room for the proposer by asking him to elaborate on his proposal. Instead of feeling angry and rejected, the proposer feels encourages.

When negative, critical remarks explode, the chairman can prevent the discussion from degenerating into open conflict by means of the following control activities:

1 Discouraging *premature* criticism of proposals. Asking members to concentrate on the advantages, and on how a proposal could be made to work, before pointing to the weaknesses and snags. Thus criticisms are not suppressed: merely made to fit into a sequence.

2 Taking a note of valid criticisms, and making sure that they are properly examined at the proper time, i.e. after the proposer's ideas have been thoroughly explored.

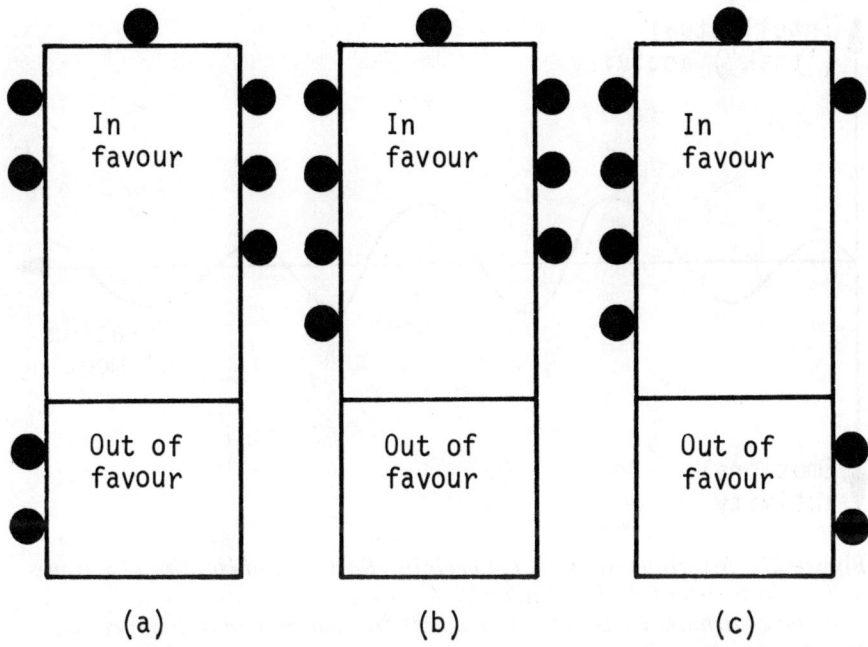

**Figure 26** *(a)    There has to be somebody on the committee who is out of favour at any one time. This is because of the group's instinctive need to attribute all its problems and tensions to a specific person or persons. (b)    But in a dynamic, developing committee roles are constantly changing, and the black sheep may move back into favour. (c)    So somebody else has to move out of favour, thus correcting the balance*

3    Soothing hurt feelings — and therefore maintaining team spirit — by:
     *complimenting* members for their contributions, and especially after they have been criticised for them;
     *praising* participants who have done extra work for the meeting, such as preparing a report or working paper or making enquiries, and now find their efforts criticised;
     *conciliating* when there is open conflict between members — for instance, by stressing the points of agreement.
Another important control activity is to maintain members' morale during the troughs which occur in every meeting (all meetings have

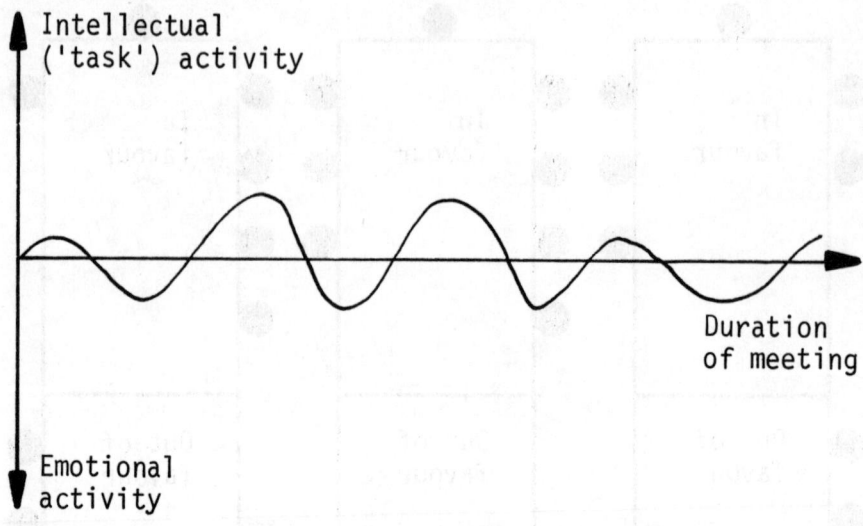

**Figure 27**   *Meetings oscillate between intellectual and emotional activity as the pressures of decision-making arouse emotions in people. That is why the chairman needs to be skilled both in 'task' and 'maintenance' leadership.*

periods of elation and depression, when members feel flat and stale). One way of counteracting depression is to throw in positive and enthusiastic remarks. Another useful ploy is to call a short break. Often when the meeting resumes, its mood has changed and members' ideas are sparking again.

Sometimes in a committee a social (or 'maintenance') specialist emerges spontaneously from the ranks and takes on himself the responsibility for encouraging and motivating the other members. This leaves the chairman free to concentrate all his energies on controlling the participation, summarising, drawing conclusions, steering members towards a decision, and other 'task' activities. It is a sure sign that this kind of task control is lacking when members are

— uncertain about objectives
— inadequately briefed
— not sure of what the next step is
— aware of a lack of direction and progress
— repeating themselves
— giving too many opinions, too few facts

The differing requirements for task and maintenance leadership are tabulated in Table 7, and the problems involved in the different

Table 7

| 'TASK' LEADERSHIP | 'MAINTENANCE' LEADERSHIP |
|---|---|
| 1 Giving/seeking information or opinions. This mobilises the meeting for the task ahead. | 1 Encouraging: showing interest or agreement; attentive listening; drawing the speaker out. |
| 2 Elaborating other people's arguments – for example, giving examples, suggesting how an idea would work out in practice. | 2 Harmonising and conciliating. Tactfully intervening to resolve conflict. |
| 3 Coordinating the contributions of several people: 'I think what both Jack and Roger are saying is...'. | 3 Soothing members' ruffled feelings when their ideas are rejected or when they are criticised. (This kind of intervention prevents psychological withdrawal.) |
| 4 Orienting the meeting by frequent summaries of progress and restatements of the objectives of meeting. | 4 Accepting people's ideas as valuable and worthy of discussion. |
| 5 Evaluation. Assessing the value of different alternatives. Estimating their practicality. | 5 Integrating new members and isolates into the committee by introducing them, tactfully drawing them into the discussion and showing an interest in them as people. |

requirements can be overcome by applying the following skills:
1   Clarifying objectives.
2   Exploiting the human resources.
3   Summarising.
4   The technique of the question.
5   Time control.

## 1   Clarifying objectives

Uncertainty about objectives breeds disorders of various kinds. The discussion seems to go round and round without direction or progress. Members talk at cross purposes or, because there is no single, over-riding goal, fragment the discussion by pursuing their own ideas and pet theories.

To avoid problems of this kind, the chairman needs to be clear in his own mind about the meeting's objectives — for instance, by discussing them in advance with one or two senior members — so that he can include a short statement about objectives in the notice of the meeting. His opening statement during the meeting should describe the meeting's purpose and powers with precision. If the meeting is one of a series, his opening statement should remind members of what has been achieved so far as well as clarifying the objectives of the present session:

> 'During our last two meetings we have tried to find ways of cutting production costs of the Spark range by 10 per cent so that we could stay competitive in spite of foreign competition. Three actions were agreed. First, to cut advertising expenditure on our less successful lines by 50 per cent. Second, to explore the possibility of substituting plastics for alloys in the casings. Third, to employ outside contractors to handle packaging and transport.

> 'It seems to me that in this third meeting we should take a very close look at our manpower situation with the aim of deciding if cuts in the labour force are possible and desirable, and where they could be made.'

After this opening statement, you may need to permit some discussion about objectives to ensure common agreement and understanding. Then keep reminding members of these objectives at intervals throughout the meeting so that everybody keeps moving in the same direction — towards the common goal.

Sometimes, though, the objectives change in the course of discus-

sion: for as you go deeper into a problem you have a sharper understanding of what is required. Thus, instead of restating, you may
need to *reformulate* objectives from time to time:

> 'When we opened the discussion it seemed that our aim should
> be to find ways of cutting the size of the labour force. But after
> considering the problems that this would create, we seem to be
> aiming at retaining the existing labour force and finding ways
> of making it more productive.'

When there are several separate items on the agenda, you may
need to open the discussion on each item with a short statement of
objectives. So by stating the objectives of the meeting, as he sees
them, in his opening statement, by allowing discussion on them if
necessary, and by reminding members about them at regular intervals, the chairman can ensure that the discussion has relevance,
progress and unity.

## 2   Exploiting the human resources

Find out everything you can about the members of your committee
— their abilities, their experience, their strengths and weaknesses.
This will enable you to 'place' them in the sub-committees where
they will be most useful, and to make sure that any assignments
stemming from meetings go to the people best qualified to carry
them out. For instance, after a meeting you may ask one member to
research costs in detail; another to report on the supply situation; a
third to investigate consumer preferences. This will give the committee the background information that it needs to reach a sound
decision — provided that these jobs are tackled by the most suitable
men.

Sometimes a problem is best tackled by splitting it into sub-tasks
and forming sub-committees to work on them. One manager I
know was a member of a committee investigating high staff turnover. The problem proved to be so wide-ranging that three sub-committees were formed. The first investigated salaries and conditions.
The second tested employee opinion. The third studied companies
that had experienced — and overcome — similar problems. In a case
like this, the quality of the committee's decisions will depend very
largely on the work done by each sub-committee — which in turn
will depend on whether its members were chosen randomly, or with
care and precision. But remember that a rapid restructuring of the
sub-committee system may be needed as new information becomes

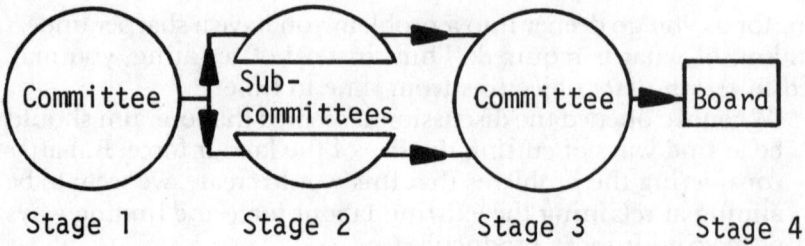

Stage 1        Stage 2        Stage 3        Stage 4

**Figure 28**   *Stage 1 — The full committee discusses the problem and decides to tackle it by splitting it into sub-problems. Stage 2 — Sub-committees are formed. Each sub-committee investigates a particular aspect of the problem. Stage 3 — Sub-committees report back to the parent committee which integrates their work and combines their recommendations. Stage 4 — The committee's recommendations are submitted to the board for revision and approval. Thus the problem is solved by a division of labour and the imposition of suitable structure*

available, as new problems emerge, or as circumstances change.

Large committees usually have to divide into sub-committees to get detailed work accomplished — and even if they don't do so formally, small groups tend to form spontaneously and do the real work of the committee. Howell and Bormann [16.3] have observed that in groups of twelve and over, a sub-group of between five and seven usually holds the discussion — the others merely sit and listen. According to Homans a leader can't control a team of more than about twelve people — the maximum number who can interact in a reciprocal fashion.

The moral is, when you find yourself chairman of a committee with membership running into double figures, form sub-committees — and select the members of each sub-committee with great care.

## 3   Summarising

Summarising is an important control activity because it stops pointless discussion, gives members a sense of progress and direction, and keeps the discussion moving forward. In any case, the meeting needs to stock-take at intervals so that it doesn't lose itself in the ramifications of the problem.

As the meeting unfolds, jot down any decisions taken, agreements made, actions proposed, and other key points. Use these notes to help you to give concise and accurate summaries of the dis-

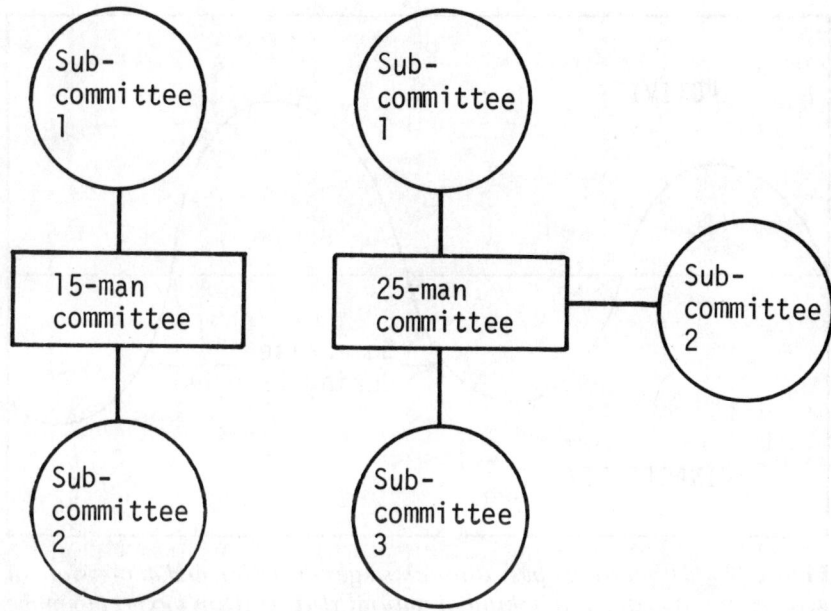

**Figure 29** *The larger the committee the more sub-committees it needs to deal efficiently with the detailed work. A chairman can't control and organise a group of more than ten or twelve members*

cussion at intervals throughout the meeting. You can also use these notes for writing up the minutes, and for reminding members at the start of the next meeting what was accomplished at this one.

As you begin to summarise, why not ask one of the members to list the key points on the blackboard or wall chart: members will then find it easy to focus on and develop the major issues.

Good timing is essential. Never summarise when the meeting is still developing a point or wrestling with a particular issue, because a summary has the effect of jerking the discussion forward a stage. Meetings rarely go on at a steady and level pace, but rather in bursts of accomplishment alternating with troughs of inactivity. So give summaries during the natural breaks or troughs:

1  During one of the inactive, depressed periods.
2  When members start repeating themselves and the discussion is going round and round.
3  When members enter their anecdotage and the meeting enters a chatty stage.

Round up the meeting with a crisp, succinct final summary. Do

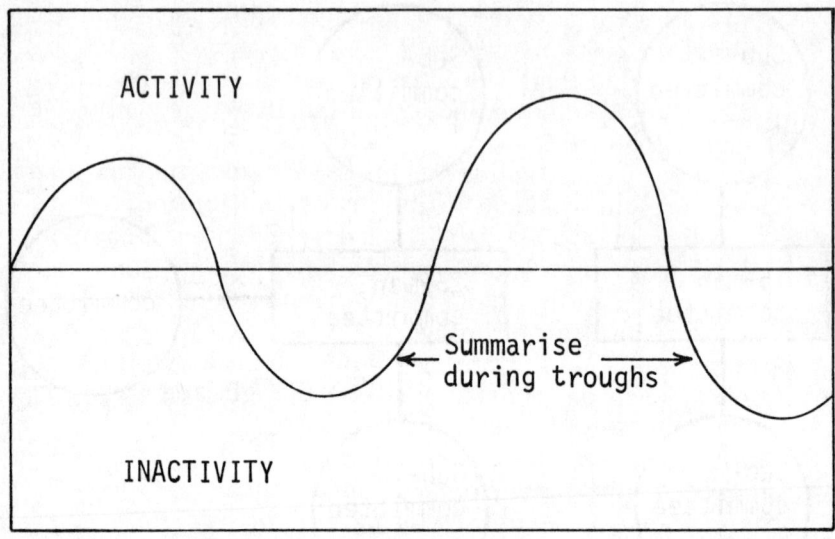

ACTIVITY

Summarise
during troughs

INACTIVITY

**Figure 30**   *All meetings pass through stages of elation and depression, of activity and inactivity, in a kind of natural rhythm. Don't expect to make progress during the inactive periods. Use the troughs as opportunities for making summaries. (A summary has the effect of rounding off one stage of the discussion and moving the meeting onto the next — perhaps more active — stage)*

this when you feel that the discussion has run out of steam and that the meeting is not going to make much more progress. Repeat any decisions or agreements made and stress any follow-up actions that are required: give a timetable of events; remind members of any letters that have to be written, enquiries that have to be made, meetings you plan to call, and so on. Thus the meeting closes decisively and members leave it with a clear knowledge of what happens next.

## 4   The technique of the question

Every chairman needs to master the technique of the question, that is, to ask questions in meetings not because he wants to know, but for reasons of control. Use the question to achieve the following effects:

1    For stimulating discussion during a slack period.
2    As a device for halting the discussion and forcing a critical assessment of some doubtful claim or shaky argument:

'We all seem to agree that it's a workable idea; but what about the costs involved?'

'You say that there would be very big savings: what kind of figure are we talking about, and exactly where would these savings be made?'

3    As a way of encouraging members to speak from first-hand experience, thus raising the quality of contributions:

'I believe that you've had a lot of dealings with this company, Jack: what impressions of them did you form?'

4    As a way of contributing to the discussion from the chair without losing one's air of impartiality:

*Assertion:* 'I don't think we should buy from Optima Supplies. Their discounts aren't good enough, and they have a bad reputation for servicing.'

*Notice how dogmatic and opinionated the flat assertion sounds when it comes from the chair. Contrast the effect when the same point is expressed in the form of a question:*

*Question:* 'What kind of a reputation have Optima Supplies got for servicing? . . . Do they give good discounts?'

One chairman became so adept at making incisive points through questions that he became known as the 'laser beam': his questions sliced immediately to the heart of the matter.

## 5  Time control

Time control is an important skill. Without it, members may spend nine-tenths of the available time discussing the first item on the agenda; or make lightning — and inadequate — decisions on complex matters; or not generate enough alternatives.

The chairman needs to exercise time control to ensure that time spent on any item is in proportion to its importance or complexity. This may require:

1    Allocating 5 or 10 minutes at the start of the meeting to the discussion of objectives and a review of essential background information.

2    Reserving 30 or 40 minutes at the end of the meeting (more if necessary) to ensure that the meeting has adequate time for assessing the alternative courses of action.

3    Imposing a time limit on each item on the agenda: 2 or 3 minutes may be all that is required for disposing of a routine matter, whereas a more important item may need to be allocated an

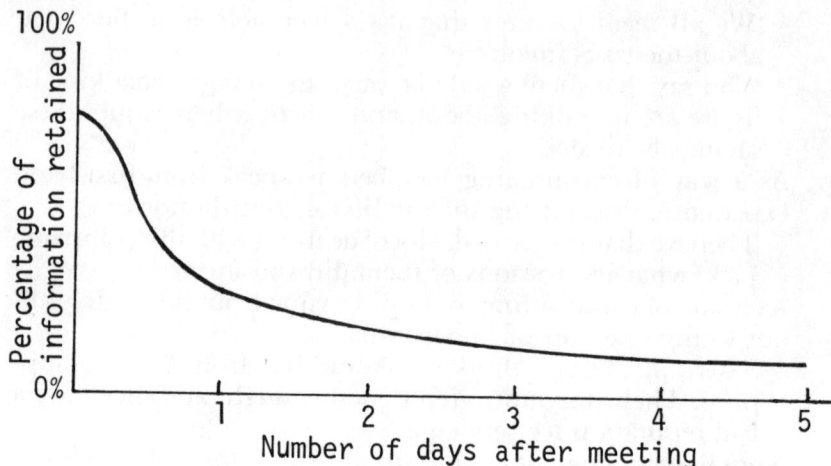

**Figure 31**   *Generally, employees prefer to receive instructions and other information in meetings (or by some other face-to-face method) because of the opportunities for clarification and questions. But, as the graph shows, people quickly forget most of what they hear in a meeting. Thus briefing sessions should be backed up with written confirmation*

hour or more discussion time.

4   Urging members to reach a quick decision on small, routine issues.

5   Preventing members from taking over-hasty decisions on important, complex matters. Most problems permit of several solutions and if the search ends too soon — perhaps because the participants are tired or because somebody is hustling for a quick decision — the optimum solution may never be born.

Don't think that your meeting can be made more businesslike simply by shortening the time available. Committees need adequate time for dealing with complex problems. So if time is limited, shorten the agenda. Remember Napoleon, who always lost at chess because he made his moves too fast.

When members are wasting valuable time, chatting or sidetracking, bring them back to the point tactfully. If a speaker rambles on and on, mixing relevant with irrelevant remarks, restate his points concisely — then ask somebody else to continue:

'I think the point that John is making is that . . . . . Do you agree with that, Eric?'

Finally, insist on a prompt start (otherwise you will have late arrivers in your next meeting); and wind up the meeting when you feel that it has stopped making progress.

*Conflict can be expressed so subtly in meetings that it is hard to detect. But to those who know the code, the lift of an eyebrow or a certain tone of voice can have the aggressive intent of a blow in the face. No matter how hard they try to conceal their feelings, the participants are grappling not only with the agenda but also with 'hidden agenda' items — the inner fears and insecurities and aggression that can disrupt the meeting and lead to poor decisions. Yet trying to suppress conflict by ruling it out of order is the wrong tactic, for this only leads to low-key meetings, a sense of boredom and over-easy compromises. More positive methods are needed.*

# 17
# Dealing with feelings

Two groups are brought into a committee room. They sit at opposite ends of the table. Red name tags and pens are given to one group, green to the other. The groups then complete questionnaires in sight of each other. There is no communication between them. Yet within minutes each group is feeling strong aggressive feelings and fears of the rival (rival?) group.

Violent emotional reactions are easily triggered off in meetings by the mere sight of somebody writing something down — or even by such trivia as somebody's hairstyle or posture or pronunciation. Fear, suspicion, insecurity, rivalry are the basic raw materials from which these aggressive feelings are made: they can prevent members 'hearing' new ideas or learning each other's viewpoints. The interior static turns the meeting into a dialogue of the deaf.

The conflict need not be crude and obvious. Indeed, it can be so subtle that only the experienced committeeman knows that it is there, acting quietly, like acid, on the group process. On the surface, all may be sweetness and light. But if you listen carefully there is the sound of heavy artillery in the distance. To those who know the code, the lift of an eyebrow can have the aggressive intent of a blow in the face. A certain tone of voice can convert a polite question into a dagger-thrust. A pause, a change of subject, a clearing of the throat, may be the only signal that the blood-letting has begun.

Too little emotion in a meeting is bad. A certain degree of tension is needed to get the best out of people. (In one experiment, two groups were given a task and told that a jury would assess the results: as a result of the tension, each group quickly developed into a tightly-knit band, regarding its own product as excellent and the other group's as poor.) But violent emotional reactions can commit a meeting to an unsound proposal or the wrong decision as members screen out arguments that don't match their own ideas, or split into camps and spend their time looking for cracks in the enemy's defences.

An observer who has seen many meetings at work through the one-way glass at the Laboratory of Social Relations at Harvard comments:

> The illusion that the group is dealing with some external problem breaks. It becomes perfectly transparent . . . that emotions have taken over and that what one member is saying does not refer at all to some external situation *but to himself.*

## The hidden agenda

Thus in most meetings members are grappling not only with the agenda but also with the 'hidden agenda' items, i.e. inner fears, insecurities and aggressions that can disrupt the meeting and disable the participants. Here are some examples of hidden agenda items from one management meeting which I observed and taped:

— Don't take me for granted, I warn you, don't take me for granted.

— You're always trying to attract attention to yourself, aren't you. Why do you do that? Trying for promotion?

— You're deliberately twisting my words again, as usual.

And there was this tense little interchange:

*Morris:* We're forgetting Item 8.

*Hardy:* We dealt with that before you came.

*Morris:* I'm sorry I was late.

*Hardy:* We missed you terribly.

*Morris:* If you go on like this, you'll finish up on the board. This kind of verbal flak hurts. It damages relationships and disrupts the meeting. Perhaps some of the exploding passions in meetings stem from childhood problems or personality difficulties. Sometimes, an observer has the impression of early hurtful relationships being re-enacted with people abusing the chairman and their parents in the same breath, so to speak. (An officer in the Marines reported how he successfully trained a platoon torn by racial and other forms of conflict, by treating them so harshly that they hated him more than they did each other; siblings united in common hatred of the father?)

In therapeutic situations recovery often follows when the patient can be persuaded to change his attitude towards his parents, siblings or others who ride around inside him like threatening spirits. But in meetings the aim is not to cure the members, but temporarily to counteract negative and disruptive behaviour so that the meeting can make a sound decision or solve the problems in a rational way. Here are three useful neutralising techniques:

## 1 Bring in an outside chairman

Often when the emotional shock-waves are running high an outside chairman can calm the storm. Inter-departmental meetings usually operate more calmly and rationally when the chairman comes from a department that is not taking part in the meeting. Typically in joing negotiations each side intensely distrusts the other, sees it as biased and closes its mind to the other's point of view. Each side tries to impose its own views, and tunes out while the other is speaking. The result is deadlock. But a chairman brought into the meeting from outside the company, or even from outside the industry, may be able to break through the prejudice barrier. For he is seen as impartial and therefore trustworthy. His comments and interpretations of each side's case seep through the mental filters and are 'heard' on *both* sides of the table. Thus mutual understanding grows and the deadlock may be broken.

When Israel and Syria began fighting in 1974, Henry Kissinger's intervention brought a cease-fire. Kissinger — the impartial and trusted outsider — acted as a kind of roving chairman to a meeting being held in two capitals simultaneously. By shuttling to and fro and explaining each side's complaints and demands to the other, he was able to bridge the communication-gap between the combatants and persuade them to stop the fighting.

## 2   *The two-column method*

Participants in meetings often fail to listen properly to points that don't match their own ideas. Or they split into hostile camps with each camp listening for weaknesses in the other's case. Ideas are classified as our's and their's, good and bad. People fail to listen properly to *all* the evidence, so judgement becomes distorted and wrong decisions are made. Instead of communication there are only ideas missing each other in psychological space.

The two-column method is useful for forcing meetings to evaluate in a systematic unemotional way. The technique, which is described in Chapter 5, forces members to make *a proper evaluation of each proposal by comparing the pros and cons, and so can boost the committee's performance.*

## 3   *Make them specify*

When people start seeing eye-to-eye because they are shouting in each other's faces, at least make sure that they are arguing about a real issue, not a whirl of air. For many disagreements in meetings are semantic — simply spun out of words:

> *Hunt:* There's a damn sight too much spending on welfare in this company.
>
> *Blake:* Nonsense. Welfare is an extremely important item and I'm amazed you can't see that. It's essential for morale. We should be spending more on it, not less.

He pauses for breath, so you smartly intervene. You ask each man to restate his position clearly, so that there is no misunderstanding. And you invite each man to give *specific examples:*

> *Chairman:* I think this is an important point. What sort of items would you like to cut back on, Mr Hunt?
>
> *Hunt:* Well, there's the sports club. We voted £5000 for it last year but only a handful of people ever use it.
>
> *Chairman:* Is that the sort of item you'd like to spend more on, Mr Blake?
>
> *Blake:* Not exactly. I was thinking more of functions like the children's Christmas party.

*Each side tunes out while the other side is speaking*

*Hunt:* Well, I wouldn't take issue with you over the Christmas party.

The chairman's refusal to let them generalise puts out the fire.

## Over-activity and under-activity

Perhaps the two most common types of disruptive behaviour in meetings are over-activity and under-activity. Thus some people in meetings are only interested in sounding good, in dominating the proceedings, in manipulating others, in constantly heckling the chairman. (It requires only a single over-active individual to wreck the meeting: the Apostles and the Knights of the Round Table were both wrecked by the disruptive activities of one man.) But participants can disrupt by under-activity, too — for instance, by refusing to argue over real issues; or by not communicating in meetings; or by conspicuously withdrawing from the discussion.

For other people, who are neither particularly over-active nor under-active, certain areas are so personally potent that they dissolve in anger whenever the meeting touches on them — such as the director of an engineering firm who used to go red in the face and start banging on the table during board meetings whenever equal pay was discussed.

Experts like Bion and Schein have identified the most common forms of emotional behaviour in meetings. They include:

> *Fight:* conflict between members which does not stem from disagreement about the proposals.
> *Flight:* avoiding contentious issues and possible conflict by too readily accepting compromise; bland behaviour, and arguments that feelings have no place in meetings.
> *Withdrawal:* a way of escaping tension or conflict or feelings of inadequacy. (The members of highly effective groups are usually skilled enough to pull withdrawers into the discussion in a tactful way.)
> *Dependency:* on the chairman or some other person in the meeting, thus seeking to avoid responsibility for making decisions.
> *Pairing:* which indicates a striving for emotional security.

Other forms of irrational behaviour have deep and twisted roots. They are extremely difficult to understand and control, even when — or especially when — they occur in oneself. Without knowing why, you feel a surge of resentment against one of the participants as soon as he begins to speak, and find yourself attacking his proposal in spite of its many merits. You reject a perfectly sound proposal because you feel obscurely threatened by it, or by the proposer. You find you have pressing business that makes you get up in the middle of the discussion and leave the meeting. And at a deeper level still, you

> may find it difficult to understand what is being said, or, sometimes, actually not hear what is being said . . . . Another sign of resistance is incoherent speech, mumbling, not bothering to make a point clear. [17.1]

When this happens, the common use of English fails to cover the frightening psychological gaps.

Thus people in meetings interact at two levels:

1   The rational level of discussing items on the official agenda, making decisions, reaching agreements, solving problems.
2   The irrational level of behaviour that stems from fears, aggressions, status-seeking, rivalries, secret power-struggles, and so on.

One of the most basic skills of managing meetings is to identify and deal with the emotional as well as the intellectual components.

*A single over-active member can wreck the meeting*

## Conflict-avoidance

Every novice chairman makes the same mistake of trying to deal
with the emotional factors by suppression. He rules conflict out of
order; takes a quick vote before the shooting-match has time to
develop; argues that feelings have no place in a committee meeting;
appeals to members to 'keep personality out of it'. But personality
insists on intruding. Feelings that can't be expressed directly get
expressed indirectly. If you have to swallow your anger against an
over-bearing chairman, your feelings will sooner or later express
themselves indirectly, in the form of clowning or cynicism or withdrawal, or some other damaging but permissible form. And these
indirect expressions of feeling are the most difficult kind to control
because the chairman is never sure what the real causes are.

It is easy enough to suppress conflict simply by ruling it out of order. This allows quick decisions to be made. But delays are bound to follow, for the members who have been over-ruled and who have had to swallow their feelings, will unconsciously find ways of resisting implementation of the decision — and so get their indirect revenge.

### Free expression

According to Brian Mitchell a healthy group is one in which members express most of their instincts in a direct way towards other members — as opposed to suppressing them or expressing them deviously. Thus it may be necessary, for the sake of a healthy group, to permit people to express responses which appear to be anarchic. As Mitchell has pointed out, frustration and repression lead automatically to neurotic adjustments within the group so that some sort of struggle is always in progress to expel somebody or to overturn the leader or to change positions, and so on.

A committee can be so afraid of conflict and try so hard to be nice, that it falls an easy prey to the first aggressive or domineering indi-

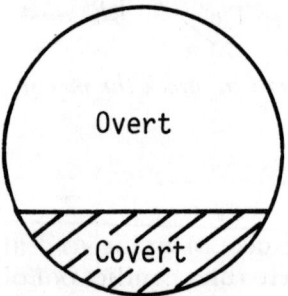
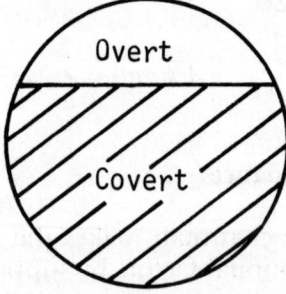

Emotions openly
expressed - so few
under-currents

'High standards' of
behaviour mean that
emotions get expressed
in disguised form

**Figure 32**   *When emotional behaviour is suppressed in meetings it expresses itself in a disguised (covert) form. This makes it more difficult to handle because you are never sure of the cause. Over a number of meetings members express the full range of human emotions, either overtly or covertly*

*Suppressed emotions make for tense meetings*

vidual who joins it: nobody likes to resist the bully-boy for fear of
friction. The other symptoms of conflict-avoidance are easy to recognise:

— Low-key meetings. Lack of involvement in members.
— A sense of boredom and lifelessness.
— A lack of disagreement about issues. Too-easy compromises
made.
— Low-quality decisions.
— Multi-solutions: decisions tend to incorporate everybody's
ideas because the group doesn't like to say no to anybody.

Suppressed emotional conflict may also be at the root of the trouble when the meeting fails to make progress, with members repeating themselves and the discussion going round and round in circles.

These are some of the reasons why, instead of suppressing feelings, you should allow or even encourage their expression — particularly in the early stages of a meeting, or early in the life of a new
committee. As Schein points out: 'Permitting and exploring emotional expression will lead to initial discomfort but will, in the long
run, produce a higher level of communication and a stronger, more
effective group' [17.2]. It may not be possible to get down to brass
tacks at once because the early stages of a new committee are, as
Schein has pointed out, a period of essentially self-oriented behaviour. The members are preoccupied with problems of influence and
status, with choosing a role, and so on. Unless you allow a period

for emotional growth — for feelings to be expressed and conflicts to be acted out — the group will be unable to concentrate on the task. Thus, especially in the early stages of a committee's life, irrational, emotional behaviour plays a necessary and constructive role.

*The discussions leading to the first decisions of a new committee are often long and drawn out. Little appears to be accomplished; yet much is being accomplished because members are learning about themselves and about each other: what they feel about each other; who is strong and who is weak; how much each man knows; what roles might be played; and so on and so forth.*

The moral is not to try to launch into the problem-solving immediately. Allow time for emotional expression and for members to find answers to pressing interpersonal questions. The only exception to this is the short, one-off meeting, where members may be able to shelve emotional problems long enough to complete their business.

## Natural development

In most meetings there are about half as many negative as positive contributions — a kind of optimum balance. That is why a lack of disagreement and conflict in a meeting is probably a sign of sickness, not health. Too much agreement may stem from an inhibiting atmosphere or a lack of involvement.

Conflict is a natural and necessary part of group process. People don't see eye to eye all the time. And it is only by disagreeing with each other that participaents in a meeting can solve problems: when there is genuine disagreement over an issue, the resulting tussle may serve to shape a superior solution. Conflict is natural, and, properly handled, it can be used to increase the range of alternative solutions. Clamorous and aggressive members can be extremely annoying: but at least they serve as receptacles for other members' aggressions and so prevent these from being deflected into the meeting.

A committee's development, like an individual's development, may be arrested by suppression. It has been suggested that all groups pass through four stages of development:

1   *Forming:* much anxiety generated because of uncertainty; dependence on the leader; a timid testing to find out what behaviour is acceptable.
2   *Storming:* conflict between sub-groups, polarisation of opinions, rebellion against the leader.

GROUP DEVELOPMENT

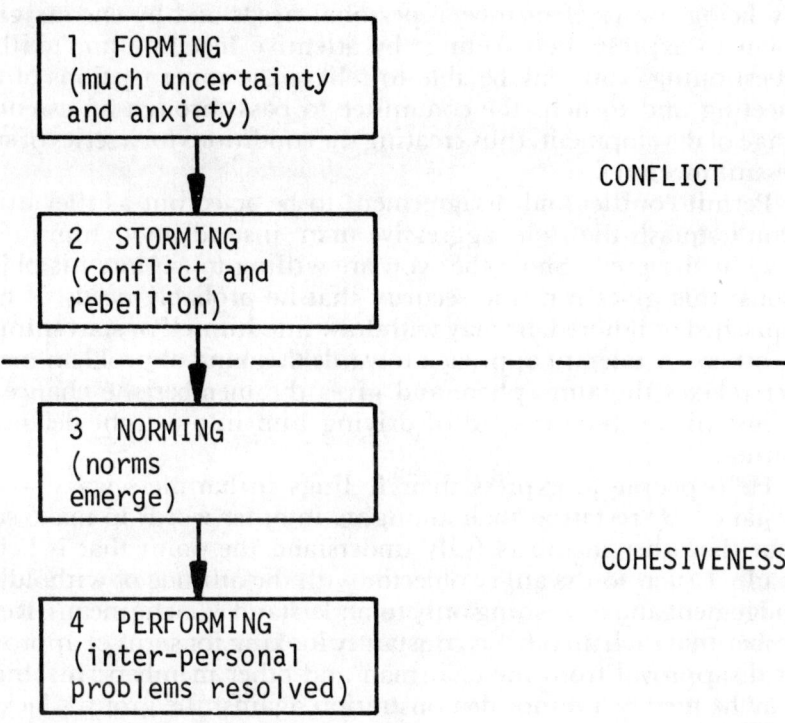

Figure 33   *Committees, like individuals, pass through different stages of development. That is why a permissive atmosphere and the toleration of conflict and 'bad' behaviour may expedite the process of group development and, in the long run, improve the committee's performance*

3   *Norming:* conflicts resolved, norms emerge, group cohesiveness grows.
4   *Performing:* inter-personal difficulties are resolved; the group concentrates on task activity.

The theory implies that before a committee can perform effectively it must pass through the first tense and conflict-filled stages. Thus permitting conflict and encouraging the open expression of feelings expedites the process of group development.

## Personal needs

By being aware of members' personal needs and by encouraging them to express their feelings by attentive listening and skillful questioning, you may be able to relieve the inner tensions of the meeting and to help the committee to pass through an essential stage of development, thus creating the conditions for a series of successful meetings.

Permit conflict and disagreement to be acted out as they arise. Don't squash the rude, aggressive man: instead invite him to say *why* he disagrees. Show that you are willing to explore his objections: this gives him the security that he probably needs. If he's squashed or ignored, he may withdraw into himself or start sniping at others. A tolerant approach towards this kind of problem member relaxes the atmosphere and gives the member the chance to adjust his attitude instead of driving him into a tight defensive corner.

Help people to express their feelings in harmless ways — for instance, by restating their thoughts in other words to make sure that the other members fully understand the point that is being made. Listen to the angry objector with the attitude of witholding judgement and of wishing only to understand what he means. Remember that each member is constantly looking for signs of approval or disapproval from the chairman and other members: his anger may be merely a minor demonstration against the group's lack of understanding. In fact, it is often a good idea to actually *solicit* objections before taking a decision — for instance, by quickly going round the table and asking each man what he thinks about the proosal. Its opponents will be happier if they feel that they have been given every chance to state their objections, and they will be less likely unconsciously to resist implementation.

## Handling the angry objector

At one meeting that I attended the chairman handled an angry objector with great skill. An Education Committee meeting was being held at a time of a national strike. The committee agreed that children should be entitled to free school meals and clothing grants in cases of hardship. A member of the committee lost his temper:

> *Chairman:* Are we all agreed then?

*Lamb:* No, we are not all agreed. It's no use trying to steam-roller us like this.

> *At this point a less experienced chairman might have reacted angrily — 'Who says I'm trying to steamroller you?' etc.*
> *Instead, he encouraged the objector to express his feelings.*

*Chairman:* Are you objecting to our helping the children of these strikers? Or do you simply object to this kind of assistance?

*Lamb:* If people go on strike, it's their own lookout. They've got to face up to the consequences. It's no use striking, then shouting out because your children are short of clothes. We've no right to spend public money like this.

> *At this stage, the chairman might have been tempted to throw in counter-arguments, sharpening the conflict.*
> *Instead, he showed a willingness to hear the man out.*

*Chairman:* You think that any hardship experienced by these children is purely the parents' responsibility?

*Lamb:* Yes I do. We've no right to use the tax-payers' money to subsidise strikes.

> *Now the chairman tried to make Lamb specify what kinds of assistance he objected to, so drawing him gently away from the emotional concept of Strikes.*

*Chairman:* Are you proposing that we should provide no assistance at all for these children. Are you against allowing them free school dinners, for instance?

*Lamb:* No I'm not saying that. We may have to provide dinners . . . .

Already the objector was adjusting his position because of the chairman's tolerant approach. The temptation, of course, is to respond to aggression with aggression — for instance, by producing crushing counter arguments, or simply by shutting the man up. But such retaliatory behaviour only deepens the conflict or, at best, postpones trouble until later.


## 'Maintenance' leadership

When a meeting is struggling to solve a difficult problem or to make a decision people inevitably get hurt. They lose arguments, have their ideas rejected, get involved in damaging conflict. Their emotions are roused and seek expression. Thus the meeting vacillates between intellectual ('task') and emotional activity, creating a kind of equilibrium. The faster the meeting drives towards its goal, the greater the amount of heat that is generated; the faster the progress the greater the tensions. The pressures of decision-making cause stresses and tensions that build up, break through, and bring the intellectual activity temporarily to a halt.* These tensions have to be dissipated before the task activity can continue.

Once a decision has been taken, however, this to-and-fro process abruptly ends: usually there is much laughter, joking and back-slapping and other signs of tension-release.

Because struggling to reach a decision in a meeting generates conflict and hostilities the chairman, ideally, should be not only a task leader who knows how to control the discussion and arrive at a decision, but also a 'maintenance' leader with the necessary social skills to soothe people and motivate them, and to maintain morale.

*Maintenance leadership means giving warmth, support and encouragement to members, thus strengthening their ability to cope with the pressures of the meeting. It means smoothing with one hand the feathers you ruffled with the other in driving towards the goal.* A useful technique for maintaining a high maintenance level in a meeting is deliberately to suspend intellectual activity every ten or fifteen minutes and to give some time to solving the morale, discipline and other emotional problems that have been generated. Here is an example from a meeting I attended:

*Peacock:* So our recommendation has been accepted?

*Chairman:* Yes. I understand that in future nobody will be appointed from outside the region.

*Collins:* It's a good ruling. But as you know, I'm the chairman of that sub-committee and I should have been informed immediately by Mr. Peacock of the board's decision.

*Peacock:* I think you're being a bit unreasonable. I heard about the decision only three days ago.

*Collins:* That doesn't matter. You've got my phone number. You've made me look a complete fool. And it's not the first time.

> *Instead of telling Peacock and Collins to 'keep personality out of it', the Chairman takes time to soothe Collins' hurt feelings and to patch the quarrel between the men.*

*Chairman:* I can see that it must have been rather embarrassing for Mr Collins to find out about the decision through a third

---

* One study of 72 committees found that the committees in which members rated lowest on socio-emotional needs got through the most business.

party. But I think you'd probably agree, Mr Collins, that Mr Peacock didn't have much time in which to act. I suppose the moral is that in future we should make sure that the chairmen of sub-committees are informed as soon as any policy-changes become known.

*Peacock:* That's a fair point.

*Collins:* Fair enough.

*Chairman:* Can we look now at the fifth item on the agenda . . . .

The meeting swings back to intellectual, task activity now that maintenance leadership by the chairman has dissipated the tension.

Often the chairman finds it impossible to be both task and maintenance leader (in a sense, the two roles are contradictory), and instead concentrates on task leadership. Very few chairmen can be both task and maintenance leaders through a long series of meetings. According to Bales, there is a one in two chance of the task leader being the most liked man after the first meeting of a group. At the end of the second meeting the chances are reduced to one in four; at the end of the third meeting to one in six, and so on. People resent direction and control. When the chairman concentrates on the task one of the members — usually the best-liked man — emerges as maintenance leader. Be sure to identify this man and treat him as an ally in controlling the committee: make sure that you and he form a mutually supportive pair.

In highly effective groups, the entire membership may handle maintenance with great skill.

## How training can help

A committee's performance can be improved by training its members to understand — and so control — the emotional life of the group. A simple but valuable training technique is for the trainer to sit in on committee meetings then discuss emotional and interpersonal aspects with the members at the end. Another useful method is to assemble people from different parts of the organisation and divide them into two groups. Each group presents a case to the other requesting some action, such as a temporary loan of equipment or personnel, or cooperation of some kind. The discussions are taped and, later, played back and analysed. Each group explains how it viewed the other's motives, how it misinterpreted and misconceived because of the aggressions and suspicions that were aroused by the interaction. Gradually, the members become aware of their own distorting hostilities and fears and the disruptive effects that these can have on the group process.

T-Group training can give deep insights into the emotional life of the group. The group is assembled and immediately left to its own devices, without organisation or structure being imposed. Without any kind of external support, the members soon present symptoms of dependency and aggression. But eventually, the group gets tired of asking the trainer for guidance — and not getting it — and converges on its basic problems: the group dynamic, interpersonal difficulties, emotional problems. In a T-Group (T for Training) members give and receive constant feedback about the impact their behaviour is having on other people. After exposure to this kind of sensitivity training, members return to company meetings with their eyes skinned to detect and counteract emotional problems.

**Inner tensions**

In most meetings, members are grappling not only with the official agenda but also with hidden agenda items — inner fears and insecurities which trigger off various kinds of irrational and disruptive behaviour (fight, flight, withdrawal, dependency, pairing, etc.). People react violently to other people. And when they are roused, what they say and think refers more to themselves than to the external situation (as the language of lovers shows) and they often take the wrong decisions.

The emotional shock-waves may be running so high that participants may actually not hear what others are saying. Asking some respected outside figure to chair the meeting can overcome this particular effect: his re-statements of each side's arguments seep through the emotional filters and are heard by *all* the participants. The two-column method is another useful technique because it forces members to evaluate all the proposals systematically and unemotionally.

Yet, paradoxically, you can't control irrational and disruptive behaviour by ruling it out of order. For suppressed feelings only express themselves indirectly; and conflict-avoidance only results in low-key meetings and low-quality decisions. A new committee should not attempt to launch on the problem-solving immediately: a period is needed for emotional growth — for expressing fears and aggressions, and for solving problems of influence and status: only after these issues are settled will the group be able to concentrate on its task. Permitting emotional expression leads to uncomfortable meetings, but in the long run it also leads to better communication and therefore a stronger group and better decisions.

A tolerant approach towards problem-members, together with attentive listening and skillful questioning, can help the group to relieve its inner tensions. Soothing, encouraging, conciliating, and other forms of 'maintenance' leadership, help the members to maintain their morale and cope with the pressures of the meeting.

*A meeting can't be considered successful when the outcomes are bad. The aim of this chapter is to suggest some ways of making sure that the outcomes are good. What is the use of making an 'excellent' decision in a meeting when the organisation lacks the resources to implement it? Or when the people affected by it refuse to carry it out? That is why the manager of meetings needs to consider such factors as what people think and where the power lies. For decisions always have to be implemented in a particular organisational context.*

# 18
# Follow-through

Usually the meeting itself is only a first step, the start of something, a mere device for triggering change; and it is impossible to gauge the meeting's success until weeks or months later, after the scenario written there has been fully acted out. At one meeting I attended, glittering plans were drawn up to transform a company's advertising policy. But nothing happened, because of sabotage by a clique of influential managers. The meeting failed to achieve its objectives because of an important factor which we all overlooked.

A meeting of department heads draws up a plan for improving communication between their departments. Later the plan is abandoned because of the high cost of implementation. The department heads failed to do their costing homework — so the meeting failed to achieve its objectives.

An operation can't be considered successful when the patient dies in the recovery room. A meeting can't be considered successful when the outcomes are not effective. The aim of this chapter is to describe some ways of making sure that the outcomes are good.

One of the first duties of the manager of meetings is to make sure that vital aspects, such as the cost of implementing a decision or the amount of support that exists for it, are not ignored in the meeting.

But sometimes a meeting gets poor results apparently through no fault of its own. An American chemical company, for instance, held sales forecasting meetings every year. For four years the meetings were successful — they produced very accurate forecasts. But in the fifth year the forecast was 124 per cent too high. The company tied down the disparity to a Congressional enquiry into the safety of oral contraceptives. But perhaps this is just another way of saying that one important aspect, one possible danger, was not properly considered in the meetings. When judged by results, how many meetings fail because of sins of omission?

Accurate forecasting is particularly difficult in high technology industries, partly because payoff on research is hard to predict — an aspect which may have to be taken into account when assessing the effectiveness of forecasting meetings. Consumer-based companies with strong brand loyalties seem to be among the easiest to forecast.

## What are the constraints?

The manager of meetings has got to know which decisions it is *possible* to make. What is the point of drawing up a rationalisation plan in an expensive series of meetings when, all the time, a majority of senior managers are solidly opposed to it? What is the point of deciding to buy new machinery when no funds are available in the appropriate budget? Be absolutely clear, well in advance of the meeting, about any financial and political constraints on the decision-making. In particular, find out the answers to these questions:

1　*What are the precise limits of the meeting's authority?* What kind of decisions can it take — or is it merely advisory?

2　*How much money is available?* Which fund or budget is the money to come from? If another committee will have to approve your expenditure, what does its chairman think about your proposals? How many of its members have you lobbied?

3　*What resources — skills, equipment etc. — will be needed to implement the decision?* Are they available within the organisa-

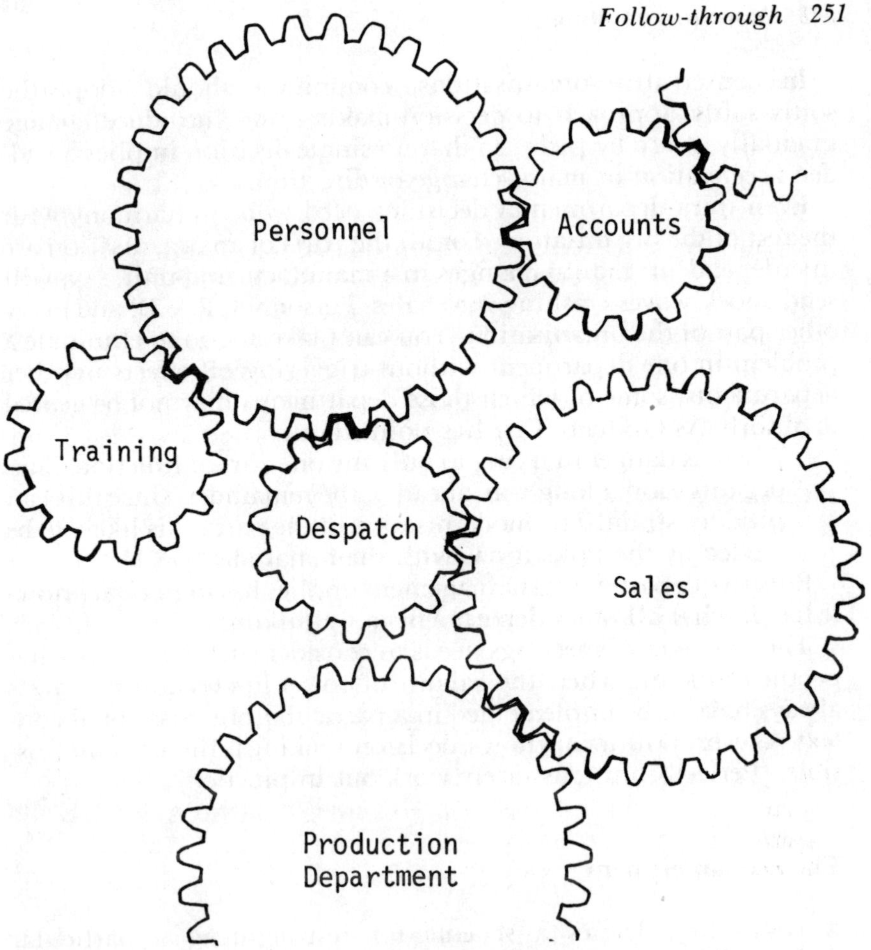

**Figure 34** *Decisions taken in one department often affect all the others. Resentment and resistance can be weakened by involving the other departments in discussions leading to major departmental decisions from an early stage*

tion? If not, have you got authority to bring in outside help?

4  *Will the decision be acceptable to the people who will be affected by it,* and to the people who will have to implement it?

5  *Will the decision be acceptable to the organisation.* For instance, in a onservative organisation, radical decisions will probably be vetoed well before they reach the implementation stage.

In conservative organisations, committees should adopt the softly-softly approach to decision-making and introduce change gradually, piece by piece, so that no single decision implies a sudden acceleration or major change of direction.

Even intra-departmental decisions need to be in harmony with the rest of the organisation. For all the parts of an organisation are interdependent: radical changes in a manufacturing unit, say, will send shock waves crashing into Sales, Personnel, R & D, and every other part of the organisation. You can't take action to eliminate a problem in one department without triggering off effects in other departments, some of which those departments may not be geared to absorb. As Graham Tarr has pointed out:

> There is danger in trying to pull any one part or function of an organisation a long way ahead of the remainder, since this can produce strain. The modernisation of the part . . . is likely to be eroded by the links it has with the remainder. [18.1]

Effective departmental management implies having a clear knowledge of what all other departments are thinking.

The manager of meetings needs to consider such factors as what people think and where the balance of power lies because decisions always have to be implemented in a particular organisational context. As every politician knows, decision-making is the art of the possible. 'Perfect' solutions rarely work out in practice.

## The human element

A committee devises a scheme for restructuring a particular division. The key proposal is to relieve a popular but incompetent department head of most of his responsibilities. The committee know about the support that exists for this man, but they under-stress it. They are more concerned about producing a perfect blue-print than about how people feel. Result: the proposals are published and a tremendous furore is created, which leaves the committee holding a perfect but unworkable plan.

In one company, a new incentive scheme was approved by a committee in the morning and explained to a meeting of workers' representatives in the afternoon. Doubts and queries were expressed which the chairman was able to answer in a rational way. Prior consultation with the representatives had not been possible because of time-pressure, but even a simple sales operation helped to reduce opposition and smooth the way for implementation.

When it is possible to discuss proposals with the people affected *before* a decision is taken in a meeting, resistance may melt completely away — especially if it is possible to integrate some of their suggestions into the final decision. If not, the simple act of expressing hostile feelings takes the force out of them.

Decision-maker and implementer, like architect and builder or conductor and orchestra, must understand each other's objectives and methods to ensure a successful outcome. But often the men who make the decisions and those who have to carry them out have quite different values and approaches, and implementation is bound to go wrong. Unless a way can be found of bridging the communication gap.

A useful bridge-building device is actually to involve the implementers in the decision-making process itself — for instance, by inviting them to attend the meetings at which the decision will be hammered out. The advantages of doing this are:

1   The decision-makers find themselves thinking and talking about implementation problems from the very start, thus ensuring a workable decision, e.g. realistic time-schedules, a clear knowledge of the resources required etc.
2   Through direct contact, planners and doers learn about each others objectives and problems. This leads to
3   A common understanding of the objectives of the decision.

Once implementation begins, why not call regular meetings of the entire project team to ensure that everybody concerned is kept up to date with progress. Key men could present short reports on the work they have done, and problems such as delays, overspending, manpower problems and so on, could be discussed by the entire team as they arose. Meetings of this kind are probably the most effective way of monitoring the progress of a big project, such as the installation of a new production process; for a number of people are always better than one person at assessing the progress of major schemes. For small projects, such as the introduction of new office or workshop procedures, perhaps the simplest and easiest method of monitoring progress and ensuring effective follow-through is for the chairman of the committee to liaise with the key implementors on a day-to-day basis, and to report back to the committee in regular meetings.

## Documentation

People have extremely unreliable memories. They forget what was said and agreed only a few days before. Precisely what was said and agreed in the last meeting *you* attended?

Once a decision has been taken in a meeting, it is unsound management to rely on people *remembering* the follow-up actions that are required. That is why, after the meeting, prompt documentation is essential. Get the actions required onto paper as soon as possible. This will help to ensure disciplined implementation of the decision. For nobody will be able to plead that he forgot something or that he was unclear about what was required. This means taking a note of the proceedings as they unfold, or delegating somebody to do this for you, so that you can circulate minutes or a short report to members soon after the meeting. This document should list any decisions taken, any agreements made and any actions required. Include suggestions — either the members' or your own — about whose help is needed, time-schedules, resources required, the way the decision should be carried out, and other useful implementation guidelines:

3    *Resolved:* That the following projects, involving estimated capital expenditure of £78,600, be started in 1976:

| | | |
|---|---|---:|
| a | Construction of new canteen | £32,600 |
| b | Levelling of the New Road site | £21,000 |
| c | Foundations and drainage systems | £25,000 |
| | | £78,600 |

*The chairman agreed to approach the head of the Plant Hire Division to request his cooperation in carrying out Project B.*

4    *Resolved:* That the new production procedures in the General Workshop, as approved at our last meeting, be introduced in October 1975.
*An early meeting with the foremen is to be arranged as their full cooperation will be required.*

## Value of a written record

The notebook used to record the proceedings will be used not only for writing up the minutes but also to settle any future disputes about what was said and when, who said it, what the alternatives were, etc. So into the notebook should go details of decisions taken, actions recommended, suggested alternatives, names of people attending, names of proposers, and so on.

If a motion is vaguely worded, say so, or suggest a better way of expressing it. Otherwise, there may be uncertainty about what was intended when the implementation stage is reached. If two or three separate motions express basically the same idea you could save yourself unnecessary labour — and help the meeting to get its thoughts clear — by suggesting a single composite motion.

Minutes are particularly easy to write if members agree to put their motions in writing and, after moving them, pass them to the chairman. The practice encourages proposers to think about precisely what they want to propose before speaking, and it ensures completely accurate minutes.

Not every meeting, of course, requires a formal record. It would be pointless, for instance, to keep a record of a gripe session where the objective is merely to give people the chance to express their feelings. On the other hand, every company is required by law to keep a written record of proceedings at General Meetings and Board meetings.

Write up the minutes from the notebook (or delegate somebody to do this job) soon after the meeting. Give each minute its own heading to help members find what they want fast. Try to get the minutes duplicated and circulated within 48 hours, while the events of the meeting are still fresh in people's minds.

## Reports

Minutes consist of a record of resolutions passed. Thus they summarise the business done at the meeting, list the actions required, provide a guideline for implementors. But the disadvantage of minutes is that ideas and arguments tend to get left out. Yet these intangibles may be the most valuable product of the meeting — a record of thinking in this meeting for development in the next. Ideas and suggestions made casually in one meeting often give valuable leads to decision-makers in some future meeting when they are recorded. Yet these valuable throwaway contributions never get recorded in formal minutes.

For these reasons you may wish to write a short report of a meeting instead of minutes. A report of a meeting should give a clear description of collective thinking, highlighting any conclusions reached, any actions agreed, any implementation methods suggested. If *disagreement* was the crux of the meeting, express this in a focused form so that people see the differences at a glance, as it were:

Three methods were suggested for increasing turnover:

(1) Price-cutting; (2) increasing sales staff; (3) setting up branches in the north and the west.

Some companies think that meetings should be recorded only when questions discussed in the meeting are left to be settled at future meetings: thus the record enables the committee to keep moving in a straight line. Other companies see the official record more as a means of communicating the decisions taken in meetings to the rest of the organisation. For instance, in one plastics company committee chairmen send tape recordings to each other. The tapes summarise proceedings, so that each committee is kept in touch with what all other company committees are thinking and deciding.

Providing appropriate documentation after meetings is an important chore, which gives the implementors of decisions useful guidelines and helps committee members to ensure continuity between meetings. Because the record of the meeting is a practical tool or memory-aid, you should be prepared to vary the format from meeting to meeting, to suit the specific needs of members and implementors. When the discussion hinges on formal motions, minutes are required. Again, formal minutes provide a convenient record of all the decisions taken when a large number of items is being covered.

But you may wish to help the implementors by writing a short report and describing in detail the kind of action that is required and suggesting ways of carrying it out.

Reports are also more suitable for meetings where ideas and arguments are more important than formal decisions. Even when a proposal is rejected, it may be useful to keep a record of the argument, so that if ever the issue is raised again the committee will be able to refer back to the report and see what its thinking and its reasons for rejection were last time.

## Post-meeting chores

Help to ensure smooth implementation of any decisions taken in meetings by carrying out necessary administrative chores as soon after the meeting as possible — writing letters, making phone calls, approaching people to request information or help, and so on. (If the committee has a secretary, these chores can be left to him.) Providing suitable documentation after meetings is especially important for ensuring continuity between meetings, and for telling the implementers precisely what actions are required.

But successful follow-through begins before the meeting is held, when the chairman finds out what decisions it is *possible* to make; the precise limits of the meeting's authority; any political or financial constraints on the decision-making; what decisions will and won't be acceptable to *(a)* those who would be affected by them, *(b)* those who would have to carry them out, *(c)* the organisation as a whole.

To reduce resistance why not arrange prior consultation with people who would be affected by a decision and, if possible, integrate some of their suggestions into the scheme. And to ensure that results match intentions, why not involve implementors in the decision-making process itself, thus ensuring a common understanding of objectives.

Once implementation begins, suitable machinery is needed to monitor progress — for instance, regular meetings of key people involved in the project so that problems can be discussed and resolved as they arise.

# References

**Chapter 1   Why meetings matter**

1.1   T. Burns and G.M. Stalker, *The Management of Innovation*, Tavistock (1961).

1.2   Eleanore Carruth, 'Sweat + Leverage = $200 Million for Arthur Cohen', *Fortune*, p136 (December 1972).

1.3   William Whyte, *The Organisation Man*, p152, Simon & Schuster (1956).

1.4   Antony Jay, *Corporation Man*, p165, Cape (1972).

1.5   D.C. Pelz, 'Some social factors related to performance in a research organisation', *Administrative Science Quarterly*, 1, pp310-325 (1956).

1.6   H.H. Kelley and J.W. Thibault, Group problem-solving', *in* Lindsey and Aronson (Editors), *The Handbook of Social Psychology*, pp1-101,

1.7   D.W. Taylor, P.C. Berry and C.H. Block, 'Does group participation when using brainstorming facilitate or inhibit creative
thinking', *Administrative Science Quarterly*, 3, pp189-205
(1958).

1.8   D.I. Marquart, 'Group problem solving', *Journal of Social
Psychology*, 41, pp103-13 (1955).

1.9   J.K. Galbraith, *The New Industrial State*, p64, Hamish Hamil-
ton (First edition 1967).

## Chapter 2    Meeting the employees

2.1   W.H. Thorpe, 'Vocal communication in birds', *in* R.A. Hinde
(Editor), *Non-verbal Communication*, pp153-4, Oxford University Press (1974).

2.2   **William Keefe, *Listen, Management*, p39, McGraw-Hill
(1972).**

2.3   *Psychology in Industry*, p172, Houghton Mifflin (1955).

2.4   James Burnham, *The Managerial Revolution*, p60, Penguin
(1945).

## Chapter 3    Management meetings

3.1   Sir Kenneth Wheare, *Government by Committee*, Oxford University Press (1955).

3.2   George Copeman, *The Chief Executive*, Leviathan House
(1973).

3.3   See P.E. Holden, C.A. Pederson and G.E. Germane, *Top
Management*, McGraw-Hill (1968).

3.4   See R. Tillman, 'Committees on trial', *Harvard Business
Review*, 38, pp6-12, 162-73 (1960).

3.5   V.A. Nazarevsky, 'A Soviet economist looks at US business',
*ibid.*, p53 (May-June 1974).

3.6   Ralph Lewis, 'Choosing and using outside directors', *ibid.*, p78 (July-August 1974).

3.7   *The Effective Board*, p7, Social Organisation Limited (1969).

3.8   *Ibid.*, p26.

3.9   Ralph Lewis, *op. cit.*, p73.
3.10  *Standard Boardroom Practice*, Institute of Directors (1961).

3.11  D. Norburn and P. Grinyer, 'Directors without direction', *Journal of General Management*, 1(2), pp37-48 (1974).

3.12  A. Jay, *Corporation Man*, p129, Jonathan Cape (1972).

3.13  A.K. Rice, *The Enterprise and its Environment*, pp59-60, Tavistock Press (1963).

3.14  C. Argyris, *Integrating the Individual and the Corporation*, pp106-7, John Wiley (1964).

**Chapter 4   Managers' motives**
4.1   Richard Nixon, *Six Crises*, p140, W.H. Allen (1962).

4.2   Chester Burger, 'Probing opinions', *Harvard Business Review*, pp35-6 (January-February 1974).

4.3   George Copeman, *The Chief Executive*, p157, Leviathan House (1973).

4.4   M. Dalton, *Men Who Manage*, p227, John Wiley (1959).

4.5   D.C. Pelz, 'Some social factors related to performance in a research organisation', *Administrative Science Quarterly*, 1, pp310-25 (1956).

4.6   Antony Jay, *Management and Machiavelli*, p215, Holt, Rinehart & Winston (1968).

**Chapter 5   A committeeman's guide to problem-solving**
5.1   Ivan Steiner, *Group Process and Productivity*, p166, Academic Press (1972).

5.2   J.L. McKenney and P.G.W. Keen, 'How managers' minds work', *Harvard Business Review*, p79 (May-June 1974)

5.3   B. Strauss and F. Strauss, *New Ways to Better Meetings*, p48, Tavistock Press (1966).

5.4   **Robert Bales, 'How people interact in conferences',** *Scientific American*, **pp3-7 (March 1955).**

5.5   R.M. Hainer, S. Kingsbury and D.B. Gleicher, *Uncertainty in Research, Management and New Product Development*, Reinhold (1967).

5.6   Norman Maier, *Problem-solving Discussions and Conferences*, McGraw-Hill (1963).

**Chapter 6   Streamline your committee system**
6.1   John Hacket, 'Ideas for action', *Harvard Business Review*, pp6-7 (January-February 1974).

6.2   Joseph Bower, *Managing the Resource Allocation Process*, p20, Harvard University (1970).

6.3   Donald Schon, 'Champions for radical new inventions', *Harvard Business Review* (March-April 1963).

**Chapter 7   Participating**
7.1   Jack Gibbs, 'Communication and productivity', *Personnel Administration* (January-February 1964).

7.2   P.E. Slater, 'Role differentiation in small groups', *American Sociological Review*, **20**, pp300-10 (1955).

7.3   Brian Mitchell, 'Towards a role theory of group dynamics', *The Voice of the Social Worker*, pp63-4 (September 1970).

7.4   W. Howell and E. Bormann, *Presentational Speaking for Business and the Professions*, Harper & Row (1971).

7.5   R.M. Weisbrod, 'Looking behaviour in a discussion group', unpublished paper, Cornell, cited by Argyle and Kendon (1967).

7.6   G.M. Prince, 'Creative meetings through power sharing', *Harvard Business Review*, p49 (July-August 1972).

**Chapter 8   How to cut running costs**
8.1   Rosemary Stewart, *Managers and their Jobs*, p64, Macmillan (1967).

8.2   C.J. Beattie and R.D. Reader, *Quantitative Management in R & D*, Chapman & Hall (1967).

8.3   Graham Tarr, *The Management of Problem-solving*, p55, Macmillan (1973).

8.4   Claude Riviere, 'He's in conference ... conference ... conference', *Vision* (February 1974).

**Chapter 9   Some common ailments**
9.1   K.C. Wheare, *Government by Committe*, Oxford University Press (1955).

9.2   Duncan Black, *The Theory of Committees and Elections*, p205, Cambridge University Press (1963).

9.3   Wheare, *op. cit.*, p5

9.4   D. Norburn and P. Grinyer, 'Directors without direction', *Journal of General Management*, 1(2), pp37-48 (1974).

9.5   C. Saunders, 'Setting organisational objectives', *Journal of Business Policy*, 3(4), p13 (1974).

**Chapter 10   Who to invite**
10.1 E.H. Schein, *Organisational Psychology*, Prentice Hall (1965).

10.2 J.R. Gibb, 'Communication and productivity', *Personnel Administration* (January-February 1964).

10.3 Don Fuller Associates, 'Reducing the risk element in decision-making', *Papers on Management*, **10**, p22 (1971).

## Chapter 11   Size

11.1 Elizabeth Sidney, Margaret Brown and Michael Argyle, *Skills with People*, p111, Hutchinson (1973).

11.2 E.J. Thomas and C.F. Fink, 'Models of group problem-solving', *Journal of Abnormal and Social Psychology*, **63**, pp53-63 (1961).

## Chapter 12   The working environment

12.1 R. Sommer, 'Further studies in small-group ecology', *Sociometry*, **28**, pp337-48 (1965).

12.2 Julius Fast, *Body Language*, p53, Souvenir Press (1970).

## Chapter 13   What's the procedure?

13.1 R. Bales, 'In conference', *Harvard Business Review*, **32**, pp41-9 (1954).

## Chapter 14   Some preparatory chores

14.1 Graham Tarr, *The Management of Problem-solving*, p44, Macmillan (1973).

## Chapter 15   Styles of chairmanship

15.1 E.E.Maccoby *et al.* (Editors), *Readings in Social Psychology*, pp522-32, Holt (1958).

15.2 Chester Burger, 'Probing opinions', *Harvard Business Review*, p34 (January-February 1974).

15.3 Richard Nixon, *Six Crises*, p148, W.H. Allen (1962).

15.4 F. Fiedler *et al.*, 'Quantitative studies on the role of therapists' feelings towards their patients', *in* O.H. Mowrer (Editor), *Psychotherapy Theory and Research*, **Ronald (1953)**.

## Chapter 16   Control techniques

16.1 R.F. Bales, 'The equilibrium problem in small groups', *in* T. Parsons *et al.* (Editors), *Working Papers in the Theory of Action*, Free Press (1953).

16.2 Elizabeth Sidney, Margaret Brown and Michael Argyle, *Skills with People*, pp114-5, Hutchinson (1973).

16.3 W. Howell and E. Bormann, *Presentational Speaking for Business and the Professions*, p63, Harper and Row (1971).

**Chapter 17   Dealing with feelings**
17.1 W. Schutz, 'Inter-personal underworld', *Harvard Business Review*, pp123-35 **(July-August 1958)**.

17.2 E. Schein, *Process Consultation: Its Role in Organisational Development*, Addison Wesley (1969).

**Chapter 18   Follow-through**
18.1 Graham Tarr, *The Management of Problem-solving*, p10, Macmillan (1973).

# Index